# PRAISE FOR SKYE JETHANI AND *FUTUREVILLE*



My friend Skye has written another terrific book. This book won't make you want to just think about what the world looks like, but how you'll shape it. It's about gains and losses and deciding to try rather than just watch.

Bob Goff, author, *Love Does*

When our country's leaders seek to plot a moral and cultural path into the future, one of the key people they look to is Skye Jethani. With *Futureville*, Skye illuminates a creative and practical way forward on some of the most challenging issues of our time. Don't miss this book.

Joshua DuBois, former director, White House faith-based initiative and author, *The President's Devotional*

In his latest book, Skye Jethani brings refreshing clarity to a vital area of the biblical narrative too often ignored or misunderstood in the contemporary church. What does the Bible actually teach about the "end of all things?" What does our eternal future really look like? And how should that knowledge inform our lives today? Skye cuts through the clutter of historical baggage and pop-theological confusion to recapture a biblical vision for our work and our lives. *Futureville* is a wonderfully lucid, profoundly impacting work. I can't imagine any believer not benefiting from this clarifying picture of our present reality—and eternal future—in the Kingdom of God.

Phil Vischer, creator, VeggieTales and What's In The Bible?

Few Christians understand and can navigate the tricky intersection of faith and culture. Skye Jethani is one of the thoughtful few. He knows that understanding the future is key to overcoming our pasts and flourishing in the present. *Futureville* is one of the most hopeful visions for discovering purpose and meaning in the here and now as we pioneer frontier of the not yet. Read this book expectantly, for it will help you unlock a life of significance that exceeds your wildest expectations.

JONATHAN MERRITT, AUTHOR, *JESUS IS BETTER THAN YOU IMAGINED*

Every Christian is called upon to work for the Lord rather than for men. In a fallen world this can be difficult. In *Futureville*, Skye Jethani sets out to reconfigure the vision of the future and applies that new vision to Christian vocation. This book is winsome, helpful, and a must-read.

ED STETZER, PRESIDENT, LIFEWAY RESEARCH

In a world that desperately needs them, Skye Jethani is one of our true public intellectuals. With *Futureville*, Skye gives us not only an honest, astute analysis of our present condition, but also a compelling, hopeful vision of the future. Rooted in a kingdom confidence, *Futureville* offers critical wisdom that will help people direct their lives toward eternity. I recommend this book to all who need to be reminded of the hopeful future that has already been won for us.

MICHAEL WEAR, FOUNDING PARTNER, VALUES PARTNERSHIPS AND FORMER WHITE HOUSE STAFFER

Skye Jethani is one of the most respected young Christian leaders of our time. This book is so deeply wise and personal that you will not just understand the worlds of faith and culture better, you will be empowered to walk a path of higher impact in both.

DR. JOEL C. HUNTER, SENIOR PASTOR, NORTHLAND, A CHURCH DISTRIBUTED

If you're like me, you're going to want to read *Futureville* multiple times. Regardless of your age or life stage, Skye offers a thoughtful, theologically-grounded view of tomorrow that will bring the hope, meaning, and purpose you need today.

KARA POWELL, EXECUTIVE DIRECTOR, FULLER YOUTH INSTITUTE AT FULLER THEOLOGICAL SEMINARY AND AUTHOR, *STICKY FAITH*

Every generation, it seems, gets gloomy and pessimistic about the future of the church. Every generation seems to see the next generation as a downgrade from the old time religion. Skye Jethani proves, once again, that the future of the church isn't bleak but is instead creative, rooted, visionary, and hope-filled. This book will pull you onward and upward, and you will enjoy the ride.

RUSSELL D. MOORE, PRESIDENT, ETHICS & RELIGIOUS LIBERTY COMMISSION

# FUTUREVILLE

# FUTUREVILLE

## DISCOVER YOUR PURPOSE FOR TODAY BY REIMAGINING TOMORROW

SKYE JETHANI

NELSON BOOKS
An Imprint of Thomas Nelson

Published in Nashville, Tennessee, by Nelson Books. Nelson Books and Thomas Nelson are registered trademarks of Thomas Nelson, Inc.

Thomas Nelson, Inc., titles may be purchased in bulk for educational, business, fund-raising, or sales promotional use. For information, please e-mail SpecialMarkets@ThomasNelson.com.

Published in association with Creative Trust Literary Group, 5141 Virginia Way, Suite 320, Brentwood, TN 37027; www.creativetrust.com



Italics added to Scripture quotations are the author's own emphasis.

**Library of Congress Cataloging-in-Publication Data**

Jethani, Skye, 1976-
Futureville : discover your purpose for today by reimagining tomorrow / Skye Jethani.
pages cm
Includes bibliographical references.
ISBN 978-1-59555-461-1
1. Christianity--21st century. 2. Theology. 3. Christian philosophy. 4. Christianity--Philosophy. 5. Christianity--Forecasting. I. Title.
BR121.3.J48 2014
230--dc23

2013025845

*Printed in the United States of America*

13 14 15 16 17 RRD 6 5 4 3 2 1

*For Manohar and Jane Jethani*

*"Hear, my son, your father's instruction, and forsake not your mother's teaching" (Proverbs 1:8).*

# CONTENTS

# ONE
# VISION

## THE PRESENT

This book is not about the future. It is about the present. It is about determining what sort of life is truly meaningful. It is about rethinking the way we relate to the world and our purpose within it. How we decide what matters today, however, cannot be separated from what we believe about tomorrow. To understand the present-shaping power of the future, let's take a journey back to the Great Depression.

For my grandparents' generation, the future began on April 30, 1939. That Sunday, scores of motorists and pedestrians streamed across the newly built Bronx-Whitestone Bridge for the first time. As they crossed the East River, behind them was the past: New York City—a metropolis under the shadow of scarcity and injustice. The Great Depression had festered for a decade and stolen much of the city's wealth and hope. But across the river, in Queens, was the promised land. Ahead of them was the future.

From the bridge they could see a gleaming white spire piercing more than six hundred feet into the sky, and at its base was its massive companion—a white globe eighteen stories high and almost two hundred feet in diameter, the largest ever built. The Trylon and Perisphere stood at the heart of the 1939 New York World's Fair and served as beacons drawing visitors across the river toward a better future. They were the starkly modern symbols of the fair's theme: "The World of Tomorrow."

It is difficult to overstate the importance of the 1939 New York World's Fair on the psyche of the country. One visitor recalled the poverty that dominated his Staten Island community at the time. "Everyone was poor, everyone looked poor, everyone ate poorly. It was a threatening, gray world, without much hope." Against this dreary backdrop, he says, "the World's Fair burst upon our lives with astonishing brilliance. Here was a whole new world set forth, a world of the future in which sheer physical plenty would be combined with grace and culture and art and beauty and technological achievement. We could hardly believe what we saw and heard. We returned again and again, reassuring ourselves that it was really there."[1]

In 1939, the nation's vision of the future had been shaped by its dismal circumstances. The Great Depression had stolen its hope. But the New York World's Fair offered an alternative vision of the future, one of beauty, order, and abundance. It kindled hope when people needed it most. The fair helped a beleaguered generation reinterpret their present maladies as a temporary condition on the journey toward a brilliant tomorrow.

What we think about tomorrow matters because our vision of the future is what determines how we understand the present. In a real sense today is defined by tomorrow. How we interpret our present suffering, our work, our purpose, even our relationships is defined by how we think about what lies ahead. The positive vision provided by the 1939 World's Fair made people reinterpret the meaning and lasting effect of the Great Depression and launched the country forward.

But visions of the future can also have the opposite effect. Consider a billboard erected by a Chicago law firm. It simply said, "Life's Short. Get a Divorce."[2] Buried in the message is a belief about the future: death is final, and there is no hope beyond the present life. This view of tomorrow also determines how to live today: maximize your pleasure, and abandon the spouse who may be inhibiting it. Today is defined by tomorrow.

These examples remind us that whoever shapes our vision of tomorrow wields enormous influence over our lives. The choices we make, the values that guide us, the work we pursue, and the people we become are all shaped by the way we think about the future. Sometimes these influences are positive, offering us a sense of purpose and hope, but they can also be damaging and cause us to be shortsighted and selfish. This is why an accurate understanding of the future is critical and why every worldview and religion that seeks to influence our behaviors has something to say about tomorrow.

Christianity is no exception. From the beginning Jesus, his apostles, and the church have communicated about the future in both word and symbol.[3] The future is an essential part of our faith and lives, because when we see the future correctly (vision), it not only allows us to transcend our circumstances (hope), but it also shapes how we live in the present (purpose). Tomorrow determines the way we relate to the world today.

This has taken on new importance as Christians debate what faithful engagement of our rapidly changing world looks like.

Studies are showing that fewer people, particularly the young, are participating in local congregations.[4] Many young adults, including those who describe themselves as committed to the Christian faith, fail to see the relevance of the local church to their lives. I spoke with one frustrated pastor about the difficulty of recruiting younger people to his congregation. "How do I get a generation that doesn't believe in commitment to commit to the church?" he asked. I believe his premise is flawed. Most of the young adults I meet are highly committed. They are devoted to their vocations, their communities, and often to social causes. They're just not committed to the things many church leaders would prefer. At a recent Passion conference for young adults, Louie Giglio captured the animating force of this generation. "The only thing we are afraid of," he said, "is living an insignificant life."

So why aren't these young people seeking significance by

committing themselves to the church and its mission? I believe part of the explanation is found in the vision of the future presented by much of contemporary, institutional Christianity, which leaves no space for a theology of vocation. We have adopted a vision of tomorrow that cannot affirm a Christian's work in the world outside the church. Instead, the message of the church being absorbed by many young people, both explicitly and implicitly, is that ministry is the only labor that really matters in light of eternity. It is a vision that tells young people most of their interests, occupations, and pursuits do not matter to God. It is a vision that says real significance can only be found by contributing time and treasure to the institutional church's work. Young people are not buying it anymore. The fault is not to be found in a generation that won't commit to the church, but in a church that cannot affirm this generation's commitments because of its vision of the future.

Younger Christians are increasingly committing themselves to social action on behalf of the poor, trafficked, marginalized, and abused. They sense God's calling to alleviate suffering in the present, but others are questioning the priority, and even the legitimacy, of such efforts. Is social justice part of Christ's work and central to our Christian calling in the world, or is it a laudable and God-pleasing pursuit that should nonetheless be prioritized below the converting of souls? One's view of the future will greatly affect how this question is answered.

Similarly, all Christians—but particularly the young—are struggling with living in an increasingly pluralistic society. Christian faith, practice, and values are no longer uncontested in the public square. But how should we approach our neighbors who follow other faiths or no faith at all? Should Christians battle for political and economic supremacy in order to impose their values upon the culture, or should they withdraw from social engagement and abandon society to its inevitable decline? If there is any ground in between these extremes, what does it look like? What is our responsibility to our communities? Again, the way we understand the ultimate destiny of our communities will shape how we engage them as well as what work within them carries eternal value.

Premise These debates around social justice, mission, cultural pluralism, and vocation can be gathered into one larger question: How should Christians relate to the world? This question cannot be answered in a satisfying manner without exploring what we believe about the future. How we live today is defined by what we think about tomorrow. For many in my generation, however, tomorrow isn't what it used to be.

## THE JADED

I saw the future when I was six years old. My parents took me to Walt Disney World, and entering the Magic Kingdom felt like walking through a storybook. But it was not pirates or castles from yesterday that captured my imagination. It was Walt Disney's vision of tomorrow.

The austere, soaring architecture of Tomorrowland was different from the rest of the park. Rather than a fantasy storybook, Tomorrowland seemed more like a three-dimensional blueprint—an attempt to predict what the future would be. Its attractions were designed to teach, not just to amuse. Mission to Mars, developed with NASA, showed us what real astronauts would encounter on the red planet, and the Carousel of Progress traced the technological developments of the twentieth century and predicted what breakthroughs lay ahead.

The climax of the vacation was a fourteen-mile monorail journey to Disney's newest attraction—Epcot Center. The Experimental Prototype Community of Tomorrow was still under construction, but the monorail provided us with an elevated preview of Future World as we circled Spaceship Earth—the geodesic sphere at the center of Epcot modeled after the giant sphere from the 1939 New York World's Fair. Just as the '39 Fair had captured the imagination of that generation, Walt Disney's utopian vision of the future captured mine. I left humming the theme song from the park: "There's a Great Big Beautiful Tomorrow." And with Disney's help I believed it.

However, Walt's vision of the future was not the only one I saw that year. On a sunny afternoon I saw another future as the lifeless body of my younger brother was recovered from a backyard pond. The shadow of death entered my world, and with it came a darker vision of tomorrow. I watched as grief, anger, and depression filled the space in our home that a toddler's laughter used to occupy. In time the pain became less acute, and the activities of my world recovered, but my vision of the world never did. Tomorrow no longer looked big and beautiful. Instead, it appeared narrow and painful. As a result, my childish, Disney-fueled optimism changed course toward adolescent cynicism earlier than most of my peers, but in time they would join me.

Their worlds were also dismantled, not usually by death, but more often by the divorce of their parents. Phil Vischer spoke about our generation's slide toward cynicism:

> Some folks believe Vietnam was the source of America's modern cynicism. Others point to Watergate. But for me and for many others in my generation, the real root, I think, is much closer to home and much more personal. When we were very young, our parents broke their promises. Their promises to each other, and their promises to us. And millions of American kids in a very short period of time learned that the world isn't a safe place.[5]

Death, disappointment, and above all, divorce conspired to shape my generation so that we could no longer believe in a "great big beautiful tomorrow." How can the future inspire wonder and hope when the world is ruled by unpredictability and pain? While suffering is not unique to my generation, the nature and proximity of our wounds are. When our parents and grandparents were children, they were impacted by poverty and war—historical forces with world-altering effects—but the environment that most shaped their identities and outlooks, their families, remained largely intact.

For those of us born in the late twentieth century, however, the dynamic was reversed. The years between the Vietnam War and 9/11 were economically prosperous and without large-scale armed conflict. We benefited from a rapidly increasing standard of living and the wonders of new technology, but our homes and families were unstable, our identities became fractured, and our outlook on the world as a whole turned dark. So, despite the end of the Cold War and the advent of the digital age, my generation has struggled to embrace a hopeful vision of the future. As Vischer noted, "Our grandparents were 'the greatest generation.' We have become the 'most sarcastic.'"[6] Rather than embracing hopeful visions of tomorrow, we mocked them. Even Disney's Tomorrowland could not deflect the cynicism of my generation.

By the mid-1990s, Disney's techno-utopian view of the future no longer inspired tourists. Research uncovered that "for the first time in recent history, the emerging generation does not share the conviction of their parents that the world is becoming a better place in which to live."[7] People went to Disney World to escape reality, but a land about the future no longer conjured happy thoughts about a "great big beautiful tomorrow." The future made people depressed and anxious. As a result, Tomorrowland became a source of great frustration within the Disney Company as it struggled to develop a new plan for the park that would not cause visitors' eyes to roll. Some within the company suggested removing Tomorrowland entirely, but in the end Disney did not abandon Tomorrowland. It just abandoned tomorrow.

When I took my own children to Disney World last year, I discovered a radically altered Tomorrowland built not on a prophetic vision of the future but on a future based on yesterday's fantasies. Using comic-book imagery from the 1950s, Disney created a caricature of the future that was part Buck Rogers and part Buzz Lightyear. The new Tomorrowland, as one Disney historian described it, mocked Walt's hopeful vision of the future "with tongue firmly planted in cheek."[8] It was a Tomorrowland befitting our jaded, cynical generation.

As we've already seen, how we think about the future shapes how we live in the present. In the case of my generation the inverse is also true: our experience in the present has shaped our outlook on the future. For me and many of my peers, broken homes, dysfunctional communities, and television-saturated childhoods have given us a cynical outlook. We grew up with parents, commercials, and political leaders feeding us empty promises that never came true. So when we encounter shiny, happy visions of the future with promises of prosperity and peace, they are met with great skepticism and even ridicule.

My generation needs more than a hope for tomorrow; we demand evidence of it today. It isn't enough to tell us that someday things will get better. We've heard that before, usually right after our dads walked out the front door with a hastily packed suitcase. We deflect platitudes about "a great big beautiful tomorrow" off our thick armors of sarcasm. For a vision of the future to have any chance of kindling life-giving hope among my generation, it must offer real evidence in the present. We demand a down payment on the future.

This is one area in which the contemporary church has

fallen short with the younger generation. As noted earlier, surveys are showing a significant decline in church engagement among the young.[9] There are many reasons, but we must not dismiss the cynicism of those born after 1970 as a factor. We are a skeptical generation, with a nose for spin and an appetite for authenticity. So when we hear Christian leaders talk about a future of peace, justice, and the end of evil and suffering—while the church is simultaneously riddled with scandal, conflict, discrimination, and injustice— we aren't going to waste our time. The label "hypocrite" quickly gets applied, as David Kinnaman and Gabe Lyons uncovered in their 2007 book, *UnChristian*,[10] and our hearts grow more calcified to faith.

Like the psychiatric patient whose paranoia causes him to refuse the drugs that would cure his paranoia, this generation's cynicism sabotages any chance of receiving the hope that might alleviate their cynicism. We are trapped in a vicious cycle, and the modern church's attempts to break through with entertaining gatherings, hipster pastors, and relevant programming have proven to be ineffective.

In order to penetrate the armor of sarcasm worn by this generation, the church will have to present a hope that isn't confined to the distant future. We must dig deeper into the Scriptures and the teachings of Jesus to discover a living hope for today. And it must be both an individual and cosmic hope that touches our personal wounds as well as the broken systems of this world—the homes, communities, and institutions where our wounds were received. Finally, we must show how this hope is being cultivated in the present, illuminating the evidence that our hope in Christ is authentic and therefore worth believing. Only when young people see glimpses of a better world emerging today will they embrace the hope of "a great big beautiful tomorrow."

## THE PATHS

The present-shaping power of the future first takes the form of hope, but there is a second way the future shapes the present—it gives us purpose. How we invest our lives, the work we pursue, and the goals we strive toward are inexorably linked to what we believe about tomorrow. In this way we are a very odd species. What other creatures obsess over their purpose or devote time and energy to deliberating what to do with their brief time upon the earth? Perhaps it is the imprint of our Creator that makes us desperately want to matter, to want our work to matter, and to frame our lives in the context of eternity. We want to pour our days into what will last, into what will endure. Moses articulated this desire in Psalm 90. We are like the grass, he said, that flourishes in the morning but withers by evening. Moses reflected on the brevity of life and the toil of our days. He concluded his song with the wish that our labor not be in vain: "Let the favor of the Lord our God be upon us, and establish the work of our hands upon us; yes, establish the work of our hands!"[11]

We desire to invest our lives in a higher purpose, in what we believe will make a difference beyond the eighty or ninety years we walk the earth. Hope, as we have already discussed, comes through an inspiring vision of the future, but we also want to know how we are going to get there. What must we do to cultivate the vision of tomorrow we have received in the present? Our sense of purpose is also rooted in tomorrow. yes

The question of purpose, how to build the World of Tomorrow, occupied most of the 1939 New York World's Fair. Visitors entering the park were drawn to the Trylon and Perisphere, the spire and sphere at the center of the park, and inside these monuments of the future they were inspired with a vision—a model of a city of tomorrow where every social evil was erased and humanity lived in perpetual harmony. Outside the Perisphere, the rest of the fair's twelve hundred acres were divided into seven zones, each focused on how to make this World of Tomorrow a reality.

Some of the attractions proved to be amazingly accurate. For example, General Motors' Futurama pavilion showed a nationwide system of highways and a future dominated by the automobile. Public support for the construction of a national highway system a few years later was a direct result of GM's display at the '39 World's Fair. Futurama was an example of a vision providing a purpose that became a reality. Yet there were other ideas that were less clairvoyant, like Elecktro, a cigarette-smoking robot developed by Westinghouse that was intended to take over domestic chores. We are still waiting. illus.

But not everything at the fair was about new technology. The Government Zone included dozens of national pavilions around a Lagoon of Nations. Apart from displaying cultural artifacts and national symbols, these government-sponsored attractions served as propaganda outposts for radically different paths to the future. For example, the United States' pavilion highlighted the advantages of free enterprise and individual liberty. Not far away was the towering pavilion of the Soviet Union—the tallest structure at the fair apart from the Trylon. It was crowned by a seventy-nine-foot statue of "Joe the Worker," representing the supremacy of the socialist society. These two superpowers, and their conflicting pathways to the future, would come to dominate the history of the twentieth century.

One nation conspicuously absent from the fair, but whose presence was nonetheless felt, was Germany. As the Nazi regime gained strength in Europe, and its sinister plan for the future was unveiled, the New York World's Fair was visibly affected. Czechoslovakia ceased to be a nation while its pavilion was still under construction, and four months after the fair opened, in September 1939, the Polish pavilion went dark as the country was invaded by Germany and the USSR. World War II had begun.

The 1939 World's Fair contains an important lesson. Even where there is general agreement about what the future should look like, there can remain profound disagreements about how to reach it. The fair presented a single hopeful vision of tomorrow but then offered different pathways to reach it. These pathways foreshadowed the turmoil that would engulf much of the twentieth century. Sadly, rather than being a century of peace and progress as the fair prescribed, disagreements about how to create the World of Tomorrow resulted in the twentieth century being the bloodiest in recorded history.

Disagreements over the best path to the future also marked my home. After the death of my brother, my parents coped in very different ways. No doubt they both longed for a future of wholeness and comfort—one in which their wounds would be healed and our family blessed, but my mother and father pursued different paths toward this shared vision.

My mother was drawn to the church. A zealous stream of evangelicalism caught her imagination with a particular emphasis on the end times. By the early 1980s, Hal Lindsey's best-selling book *The Late Great Planet Earth* had convinced millions of Christians that Christ was coming soon to rapture them away from the pain and evil of this world.[12] I can understand the appeal of this message for a mother grieving the loss of her child. My father, on the other hand, distrusted what he called "organized religion." His path forward was self-discipline and hard work. He was a physician, and he worked tirelessly to build his medical practice to ensure a better future for himself and his family. He could not erase the pain of the past, but he could strive to build the future he wanted.

Like the 1939 World's Fair, the divergent paths in my home resulted in conflict. Not just personal conflict between my parents, but a conflict of purposes. My brother and I were left to make sense of conflicting messages about what mattered most. What should we give our lives to? Faith or finances? Religion or education? Work or worship? Which path would lead us toward a future of wholeness and peace? What kind of life really matters? Of course, these are not questions unique to my adolescence. They are ones I come across frequently among the college students I have mentored and taught. They want to know what to do with their lives. They want to invest themselves in what matters most. But how do we determine what that is?

Since the beginning of Christianity, questions of significance have been linked to eternity—that which is eternal is what matters. Jesus tells us not to value what is temporary at the expense of that which is eternal. "Do not lay up for yourselves treasure on earth, where moth and rust destroy and where thieves break in and steal, but lay up for yourselves treasures in heaven, where neither moth nor rust destroys and where thieves do not break in and steal."[13]

Investing our lives in treasure that will not be destroyed means determining what we believe to be eternal, what will endure. Again, our vision of the future shapes our actions in the present. In some Christian communities we are told that all creation, apart from the souls of the redeemed, will be destroyed and replaced. This view has serious implications for what we determine to be a meaningful life. Why invest your energy in designing beautiful, efficient, and safe buildings if they're destined for the flames? Why compose music, develop just governments, or seek to eradicate a deadly virus? In communities that hold such a view of the future, it makes sense why ministry, narrowly defined as rescuing and restoring souls, becomes the all-encompassing purpose of the Christian life. They don't believe anything else will last.

What does the church have to say to the great majority of

Christians who are called to work other than ministry? Does it have a message other than, "Do your work ethically," "Share your faith with your coworkers," or "Give your earnings to missions"? These responses do not answer the angst of a generation desperately seeking significance. Any meaningful answer will require the church to reexamine how it thinks and speaks about the future. We owe it to them, and to all followers of Christ, to see if our view of the future conforms to what Christ and his apostles taught. Getting it right will provide people a sense of purpose and dignity in their work, but getting it wrong will steal it from them.

## THE FUTURE

I wrote my previous book *With*[14] because I have grown increasingly concerned that those within the church are being inoculated to the gospel, that they are being taught a way of relating to God contrary to the message of Christ. As a result, they are approaching God from a posture of control predicated on fear, rather than one of faith flowing from love. How we relate to God, however, is only one side of the Christian life. As Jesus taught us, the greatest commandment is to love God and the second is like it, to love our neighbor.[15] Throughout the New Testament, these two facets of Christianity, love for God and love for others, are presented as inseparable. As John wrote, "He who does not love his brother whom he has seen cannot love God whom he has not seen."[16] So I have always felt *With* was an important but incomplete book. Getting our relationship with God right must find its completion in how we relate to those around us.

That is my desire for this book. Not only must we reimagine the way we relate to God, we must also reimagine the way we relate to the world. Should we retreat from the destructive evils of our society to create safe enclaves until Christ returns, or should we storm the walls of our cultural institutions and take them over with policies and legislation rooted in biblical ethics? Are we to give ourselves fully to the numerical growth of the local church, or should we be focused on the alleviation of physical and temporal suffering? Does it matter whether we are cooks or clerics, missionaries or mechanics? What kind of work really matters, and how does our communion with God manifest itself in this world?

As I have reflected on these questions, my mind is always led to the same place—the future. As Christians, we believe that a meaningful life is one spent participating in what God is doing—God's mission. But the scope of God's mission is defined by what we believe the future looks like, by what will endure. So we cannot begin to define how we should live in this world without exploring what we believe about the world to come.

We have seen in this opening chapter how our sense of hope and purpose in the present is the product of our vision of the future. Some outlooks cultivate life-giving hope and a clear sense of meaning in our lives. Others can rob us of hope and cause us to live a narrow, selfish existence. We have also identified the particular challenges facing the present generation. Our cynicism has made us resistant to hope, yet we remain fearful of living insignificant lives. In addition, our culture, including within the church, presents us with different and sometimes contradictory paths to the future. How do we know which to walk?

Like the beleaguered New Yorkers who crossed the East River looking for hope and purpose amid the Great Depression, I invite you to leave behind your present reality and join me as we explore a vision of the future. As your vision of Futureville becomes clearer, I trust it will inspire you with hope and purpose for your life today.

# TWO

# CULMINATION

## THE ASCENT

As the poor, huddled masses entered the 1939 New York World's Fair, they were drawn to the colossal, white tower and globe at its center. Although they appeared futuristic, the Trylon and Perisphere were inspired by artwork created much earlier. *Within the Gates*, an engraving by artist A. I. Rice created in 1875, was his vision of heaven: a garden city dominated by a flawless, white sphere and triangular tower. Designers of the World's Fair copied Rice's heavenly vision and placed his Trylon and Perisphere at the center of the park to symbolize the paradise they hoped the future would be—but they were more than symbols.

Once beneath the eighteen-story sphere, visitors stepped onto the world's tallest escalator. It lifted them into the air and through a doorway. Like the apostle John being called up to heaven to receive a vision of the future,[1] visitors to the World's Fair ascended into the Perisphere for a glimpse of the world of tomorrow. Once inside, they rode a moving balcony across an artificial sky and peered down upon a model of what was touted as "a perfectly integrated garden city of tomorrow." For six minutes an invisible narrator spoke about the utopian world of 2039, where the citizens lived in a leisurely community mixing the best of urban and rural life known as Pleasantville. The scene was a striking contrast to the slums and tenements choking Depression-era New York. When finished, visitors exited the Perisphere via a gradually sloping 950-foot ramp wearing pins declaring "I Have Seen the Future."

In this chapter I want to take you into the Perisphere to catch a glimpse, not of an American Pleasantville, but of a Christian Futureville—the name I've given to the world of tomorrow espoused by Scripture.

From its inception, Christianity has been a faith focused on the future, and today there continues to be widespread fascination about the end times, or what theologians call *eschatology*—the study of last things. Fictional novels on the subject have become best sellers, and pop Christianity seems preoccupied with predicting when the end will come. With so much interest has come a great deal of confusion and, to put it plainly, bad theology. As some scholars have noted, popular beliefs about the future usually tell us more about the people and culture from which the belief emerges than anything meaningful about the future itself. I believe this is largely because we have divorced the Christian vision of the future from the larger story of Scripture to which it belongs.

When we speak about the future, any future, we are really talking about upcoming chapters in a story still being told; if we are to accept these unread chapters, we must be familiar with the story they complete. For example, when the visitors to the 1939 World's Fair entered the Perisphere to see Pleasantville, they were prepared to receive the vision as the culmination of a narrative they already knew. Americans had accepted that they were part of an unfolding story of human progress, freedom, and industry. To remind them of these preceding chapters, the boulevard leading to the Perisphere was lined with the symbols of the American narrative—a statue of George Washington, sculptures representing constitutional rights, and other icons of American business, art, and history. Entering the Perisphere was then a way of previewing the glorious climax of the American story already underway.

Likewise, before we can enter our Perisphere and glimpse the culmination of the Christian story in Futureville, we must first put the future into context. While volumes can be written, and have been, about the biblical narrative of the world, we will retrace the story with two simple metaphors: the garden and the wilderness.

## THE GARDEN

The ancient Hebrews viewed the sea as a dark, foreboding abyss of chaos—an ominous realm that stood in contrast to their

God of order. Their Scriptures began with this God creating order out of a primordial abyss:

> In the beginning, God created the heavens and the earth. The earth was without form and void, and darkness was over the face of the deep. And the Spirit of God was hovering over the face of the waters.[2]

From the churning waters God called forth order. He separated sky from sea, land from ocean, darkness from light. He formed an organized world in the midst of a cosmic wilderness. Then he carved out one place to be unlike any other—a place where his will, intention, and purpose would be exhibited most clearly. God created a garden:

> The Lord God planted a garden in Eden, in the east, and there he put the man whom he had formed. And out of the ground the Lord God made to spring up every tree that is pleasant to the sight and good for food.[3]

This patch of real estate in Eden was intended to be the ideal habitat for humans, with everything necessary for us to flourish. This first garden was marked by three characteristics: order, beauty, and abundance.

Order is what makes a garden a garden. A jungle or forest may be beautiful and full of life, but neither is tended. They are random, self-regulating ecosystems. A garden, on the other hand, requires a gardener. Eden did not arise randomly. God planted it, and he "made to spring up every tree." By its very definition a garden is a place of order and purpose. The garden of Eden represents the realm in which God's fullest intent was made manifest.

We are also told, "God made to spring up every tree that is pleasant to the sight." Early Jewish theologians did not miss the fact that the writer of Genesis listed the trees' beauty ahead of their usefulness, and this beauty came in diverse expressions. The fact that "every" beautiful tree was made to grow in Eden celebrates the abundant diversity of beauty God has created. Although it is often dismissed as nonessential, Scripture affirms that humans require beauty to thrive. Beauty nourishes our spirits the way food nourishes our bodies.

The garden also contained everything the man and woman needed to thrive physically. It was a place where resources existed in abundance. The trees offered food that was good to eat, four rivers supplied water, and there was no threat of starvation, depletion, or decay. Simply put, there was always enough.

If we ended the exploration of the garden here, the image would conform to popular assumptions that Eden was a place of relaxation and carefree living—the ultimate all-inclusive resort. But Eden was not the Creator's idea of a perpetual vacation. Genesis says, "The LORD God took the man and put him in the garden of Eden to work it and keep it."[4] The man wasn't a pampered guest in Eden; he was the manager and maintenance man. God had put humanity in the garden to be his representatives; they were created to be his image-bearers in the world and to have dominion over the earth.[5] In other words, humans were created to rule and govern this new world with God. The man began this task by naming the animals, which itself is an act of creation—a way of organizing and categorizing. He was cultivating more order.

Some mistakenly believe that Eden was a self-contained habitat, a divine zoo in which God planned to confine his human creatures for his own amusement. In truth Eden was more like a base camp from which the man and woman were to expand God's garden to encompass the entire earth. He told them to "fill the earth and subdue it."[6] In communion with God, humanity was to extend the order, beauty, and abundance of Eden to the ends of the earth. This good work was our intended purpose as the image-bearers of God.

It might sound like a difficult and laborious job, hardly a leisurely paradise; but that is because you and I exist in a universe that strives against our efforts. Creation itself resists our attempts to build, order, and create. But the first humans, according to the biblical narrative, knew no such resistance. They lived in perfect harmony with all creation. The world wanted to submit to them. The work to extend the garden was not a contentious striving against a stubborn cosmos but a joyful endeavor that drew upon the creative impulse and inquisitiveness that God had put within his image-bearers.

The ancient Israelites described this harmonious ordering of creation in which humanity flourished as *shalom*. The word is commonly translated as "peace," but that only captures one facet of its meaning. Shalom is the peace that comes from wholeness—from lacking no good thing and living in harmony with God, creation, and one another. It is the condition that produces comprehensive flourishing, where everything and everyone fulfills their God-intended potential. This was exactly the condition of the man and woman in the garden. They had a purpose, they enjoyed endless variations of beauty, and they had abundant resources. In addition, they possessed perfect unity with each other and their Creator. God was with them. Together they would rule over the world in endless wonder and delight as the glories of each new expression of order and beauty they created outshone the previous. Until it all went wrong.

## THE WILDERNESS

I would not describe my experience in this world as one of ceaseless order, beauty, and abundance. Few would. Rather than a garden of shalom, the world we know appears to be a dangerous wilderness. We anxiously search for meaning and order in a cosmos some have concluded is incapable of providing it. We wrestle daily against the ugliness in the world, in our communities, and within ourselves. We are driven by the fear that we won't have enough—enough food, wealth, safety, or days left to enjoy them. And rather than delighting in an endlessly creative existence in unity with God, we look upon the suffering in this world and doubt whether a benevolent Creator even exists.

How did the garden of shalom become a wilderness of fear?

The biblical narrative tells us the garden was lost when humanity rebelled against God. Rather than living and ruling with him, we sought to be over him. In a story familiar to many, a serpent deceived the man and woman into eating the fruit of a tree God had forbidden them to eat from. They did not take the fruit merely because it was appetizing. They ate because they wanted to "be like God."[7] It was an act of rebellion—a rejection of God and his plan to rule the earth together. They no longer wanted to be with God. They wanted to be gods.

This rebellion triggered a disastrous chain reaction that shattered the shalom of creation and fundamentally changed the ordering of the cosmos. The first evidence was an unfamiliar stirring within the man and woman—fear. In a garden of perfect order, beauty, and abundance, fear was unknown and unnecessary. But as the order God had created began to deteriorate back into chaos, the perfection of creation was undone, and fear spread like a contagion. Scripture uses a single word to describe our rebellion against God and its dreadful repercussions: sin.

Following their coup d'état, the man and woman were sent out of Eden into the wilderness. Although often interpreted as a punishment for their sin, we must not forget that God always intended for humanity to leave Eden. They were given the mission to cultivate the entire earth to reflect the order, beauty, and abundance of Eden, and they still carried this instinct after falling into sin. But having rejected God, they would now pursue this work without him, surrounded by a creation that would no longer willingly submit to their efforts. So as they left

Eden and entered the wilderness, the land of shalom was lost, and the road back was blocked.

Thereafter humanity would know only the harsh wilderness of the world. Where the garden was a place of order, the wilderness was ruled by chaos—unpredictable and devastating events assail us without warning. Where the garden was a realm of beauty, the wilderness was dominated by ugliness—flowers fade and the grass withers; decay and death are the way of all things. Where the garden provided abundant resources, the wilderness was ruled by scarcity—we must strive and toil to acquire what we need to survive, and this often leads to conflict between individuals and communities. These broken aspects of the world provoke within every person what it provoked within the first man and woman—fear. We are all afraid.

Because we see the world as an unpredictable, threatening wilderness, we live with a ceaseless desire to protect ourselves. We seek to mitigate our fears by striving for control over our world and those around us, and control requires power—the very thing that humanity selfishly pursued and that landed the world in this broken condition. Power itself, we should note, is not evil. God granted power in the form of authority to the man and woman in the beginning when he called them to "subdue" the earth.[8] The evil came when they were not content with this power and instead sought God's power for themselves. So we now find ourselves trapped in endless cycles of fear and control, of feeling powerless and desperately grasping for more power. This is why Friedrich Nietzsche concluded,

"The world itself is the will to power—and nothing else! And you yourself are the will to power—and nothing else!"[9] The destructive pursuit of power, fueled by fear of a dangerous world, can explain a great deal of human history, but it cannot explain everything.

Despite the nihilist perspective of Nietzsche and other atheists, God has not abandoned his creation to sin and evil. He is not a Creator who rejects and replaces; he reconciles and redeems. The story of Israel in the Old Testament is the story of the Creator beginning a plan to cultivate a new garden within the wilderness of the world, to once again bring order, beauty, and abundance to his creation. Binding himself in relationship first to Abraham and then to his descendants, God's presence with his people is marked by the restoration of the garden.

The central narrative of Israel's story shows this. In the exodus story, God called his people out of slavery in Egypt and led them into a literal wilderness, but his presence transformed the wilderness into an oasis—a garden surrounded by a hostile environment. First, God established order by leading his people by a pillar of cloud by day and fire by night. They were not abandoned to chaos but guided by the "mighty hand and an outstretched arm" of God.[10] Order is also established as God gave his people his Law—the guidelines for their lives, worship, and community. The righteousness of this Law, its divine order, was what distinguished Israel from all the peoples of the earth.

In the arid ugliness of the Sinai desert, God also cultivated beauty. He commanded them to build a mobile place of worship, and the people were filled with his Spirit to create beautiful things of gold, silver, stone, metal, and fabric to accomplish the task.[11] The tabernacle was decorated with garden images and stood at the center of the community as a reminder of Israel's God, but its most beautiful feature was not created by human hands. Upon completion, "the glory of the Lord filled the tabernacle."[12] The beautiful presence of God himself radiated from the tent.

Finally, the Israelites experienced miraculous abundance in the wilderness. In that dry and deadly land, God caused streams of water to flow from rocks; he transformed rancid pools into clean, sweet water. He caused bread to fall from the sky each day to feed his people, and he guided flocks of quail to their camp for meat. And during their forty-year sojourn in a region with few natural resources, God ensured neither their clothes nor their shoes deteriorated.

Through this, the Israelites learned that the wilderness of the world could be transformed through the power and presence of God. Despite living in a world marked by chaos, ugliness, and scarcity, they did not have to be afraid because God was with them. Shalom could still be cultivated in the world through the grace of Israel's God.

The examples of God's transforming presence continue throughout the Old Testament, but the message is not limited to Israel. The fact that we, too, catch glimpses of order, beauty, and abundance in our fallen world is evidence that God has not abandoned us. Yes, our world is a dangerous and scary wilderness, but the echoes of Eden have not been entirely lost.

G. K. Chesterton compared our world to a cosmic shipwreck. We are like sailors, he said, waking up on the beach with amnesia. As we wander the shore, we discover gold coins, precious cargo, a compass, and other valuable remnants from a civilization we can barely remember. Similarly, we catch glimpses of an earlier world that we've long forgotten. Beauty, joy, love—these things catch us by surprise in our broken world and stir our hearts. They remind us of the world we were created to occupy and ignite a longing for a future world we hope to attain. This longing is so strong, so universal, that we will go to extraordinary lengths to catch glimpses of God's garden even in the most oppressive wildernesses of this world.[13]

During the Nazi oppression of Poland, young Gerda Klein spent months hiding with her family in a cellar. Despite the danger, she would sneak out to visit a garden she called "my paradise." She longed "to be in touch with nature, growth and beauty." Eventually, the Germans caught her and imprisoned her in a work camp in Grünberg—a brutal place Klein described as "cruelty set against a background of beauty." In the Nazi work camp, two thousand girls marched each morning to the factory through a courtyard with beds of roses and tulips. "Day after day," said Klein, she "had to resist the desire to run out of line and touch those beautiful blossoms." One morning, when a single crocus had sprouted through a crack in the concrete, the parade of young slaves silently parted as "hundreds of feet shuffled around it" to avoid trampling the flower.[14]

Our lives in the world are marked by cruelty, but they are set against a background of beauty that remains frustratingly beyond our touch. We still desperately seek evidence—even the smallest glimpses—that the world we long for will someday be within reach. Even in the most unyielding wildernesses, we look for signs that the garden is real, that it will not remain forever beyond our grasp, and that someday we will be free to run out of line and take hold of the beauty our spirits crave. We all journey through the wilderness of the world with the echoes of Eden in our souls.

## THE CITY

The narrative of Scripture is a long, twisting story, and my goal has not been to capture all, or even most, of its peaks and valleys. (We will be exploring much more of it in the chapters to come.) My intent has been to trace the general arc of the Christian story so that our view of the future can be perceived in its proper context. It is to this future we now turn our sights.

Having recounted the story of creation's garden and rebellion's wilderness, imagine ascending into the Perisphere for a preview of Futureville, the final chapter of this cosmic saga. What might you expect to see? Like every story, we want to see good triumph, the hero win, and a soul-satisfying resolution of the conflict. So within the Perisphere we might expect to see a world restored to the qualities first seen in Eden—a world of order, beauty, and abundance in which humanity is delivered from fear and evil. We might expect to see a return to the garden of creation. If the Christian story culminated this way, it would be a cyclical narrative in which the end is really a return to the beginning, like many popular movies where the protagonist awakens to discover his struggle was nothing more than a nightmare and all is right with the world. Some hold to this understanding of Christianity. They believe God intends to press a Reset button on the cosmos, reboot his creation, and start over. They believe in a restoration narrative.

But entering the Perisphere, that is not what we find. We do not discover a return to Eden. In fact, we do not find a garden at all. Instead, we gaze upon a city. In the final book of the Bible, the apostle John was given a vision of the age to come—a peek at the culmination of the Christian narrative. He did not see Eden restored, but rather a city descend:

> And [the angel] carried me away in the Spirit to a great, high mountain, and showed me the holy city Jerusalem coming down out of heaven from God, having the glory of God, its radiance like a most rare jewel, like a jasper, clear as crystal.[15]

Why does the Christian story culminate with a city and not a garden? To answer that we must shed our modern assumptions and see through the lens of the ancient world. Attitudes toward cities profoundly shifted after the Industrial Revolution in the nineteenth century. Thanks to factories and rapid urbanization, people came to view cities as congested, polluted trash heaps of humanity riddled with disease and crime. As a result, a romantic vision of nature emerged at this time. People flocked to parks and forests to escape the brutality of urban environments, and nature was glorified as a pristine sanctuary untainted by the ugliness of man.[16] But in the ancient world, well before the Industrial Revolution, attitudes were quite the opposite. Most people viewed nature as a threatening and brutal place to be avoided, and cities were seen as enclaves of safety and civilization where art, industry, government, and commerce thrived. To the ancients a city was a refuge from the surrounding wilderness; it was a garden where order, beauty, and abundance had reached their full flourishing.

So John's vision of a city in Revelation 21 is both a return to Eden's qualities and a fulfillment of Eden's potential. If you recall, God's original intent for humanity was to "fill the earth and subdue it";[17] he called his image-bearers to carry the order, beauty, and abundance of Eden throughout the world until the earth fully reflected the qualities of his garden. What we discover in John's vision, then, is the world God always intended. It is the mature world humanity should have cultivated with God had they not rebelled and allowed evil to pervert creation. John's vision is not a return to Genesis; God does not push a Reset button on the universe. Unlike so many other ancient myths, the Christian story is not cyclical; it is definitively linear. It progresses to a glorious and surprising culmination.

Imagine a master painter working on a great mural with his apprentices. Having started the painting and outlined the design, the master leaves. The apprentices, having contempt for the master, erase his design and make a mess of the mural by throwing paint on the wall. When the master discovers their destruction, the apprentices believe he will be forced to start over. When the master returns, however, he does not despair. Instead, he finds a seam at the edge of the mural and begins to pull away a layer the apprentices had not seen. As the mask separates from the wall, some of their paint is lifted away and destroyed, but remarkably, some of their paint remains and is incorporated into the composition. When the mask is fully removed, to the astonishment of the apprentices, the completed mural the master had always envisioned is revealed. What they had intended for evil was transformed by the master into good.

Likewise, what Revelation shows is beyond what we expect. When evil infected creation in Genesis 3, we assumed God's plans had been thwarted, that he would have to deconstruct his world, clean up the mess we created, and start over. But John offers us a different end to the story. The unveiled city represents the world God always intended. His plan has not been derailed; his masterpiece has not been destroyed; he does not start over. Instead, we discover that God has triumphed, and his goal has not been impeded despite evil's best attempts.

A closer examination of Futureville offers even more clues about the world of tomorrow. John described the massive metropolis as "pure gold"[18] with cubic dimensions—equal in length, width, and height. The symbolism would not have been lost on his first-century readers. The innermost sanctuary of the Jewish temple, known as the Holy of Holies, was where God's presence was believed to dwell. The room was inaccessible to anyone but the high priest, and he was permitted entrance only once a year on the Day of Atonement. It was a perfect cube-shaped space with every surface covered in gold. John was telling his audience that in the age to come the Holy of Holies, the abode of God, would be shared by his people; the whole city is now a sanctuary:

> And I heard a loud voice from the throne saying, "Behold, the dwelling place of God is with man. He will dwell with them, and they will be his people, and God himself will be with them as their God."[19]

The unity shared between God and humanity at the beginning in the garden will be restored.

The fear that dominates our experiences in the world's wilderness will also be gone. That ancient symbol of chaos, the sea, John said is no more,[20] and the city is surrounded by a great wall with twelve gates that are never shut because there is no danger. Order again rules over the cosmos. We will not have to be afraid.

Through the open gates the nations bring their glory and honor. They populate the city with the most beautiful artifacts of human culture, but these glories cannot compare to that which radiates from God himself. John said the city has "no need of the sun or of the moon to shine on it, for the glory of God has illumined it."[21] The city will be a place of unimaginable beauty.

Within the city, straddling a river, will be the tree of life first mentioned in Eden. The way to this tree, which had been closed after the rebellion of the man and woman, is now opened. Its fruit and leaves will be without end, and they will bring healing to the nations. As John wrote, "There will no longer be any curse."[22] Abundance, rather than scarcity, will mark this new age.

While some will argue for a literal interpretation of John's vision of the future, placing his revelation within the larger context of the biblical narrative should help us see his deeper intent. Will a giant, gold, cube-shaped city someday descend from the clouds, dry up the oceans, and feed all people from a single tree? I don't believe that is John's message. These symbols are clearly targeting the imagination of his first-century audience in order to communicate a more profound message. John was revealing a coming age where God will again dwell with his people and the cosmos will be put right. Chaos, ugliness, and scarcity will be displaced by perfect order, beauty, and abundance. The world of tomorrow will not see Eden merely restored but also fully matured.

## THE DESCENT

Every vision must end. Eventually John's revelation dissipated, and he returned to his exiled existence on the island of Patmos, where he wrote down his vision to encourage the church. Ever since, Christians have been interpreting his words and wondering how the city of the future he saw would come to pass. Like John, after receiving their vision of tomorrow, the visitors to the 1939 World's Fair eventually exited the Perisphere. They slowly descended back to earth to explore the rest of the fair and discover how Pleasantville would be made a reality. Now it is our turn to do the same. We must leave the Perisphere and discover the path to Futureville.

While many may agree with the culmination of the Christian story presented in this chapter, how we get there is a different matter. Even among Christians, there remain stark differences over which path will lead us to Futureville. The path we choose is important because while all roads to tomorrow promise us hope and purpose, not all can deliver them. Rather than leading us closer to the garden city, some prove to be primrose paths that take us further away. Instead of order, beauty, and abundance, they lead the world into deeper chaos, ugliness, and scarcity. The next chapters explore three pathways to the future and how they either frustrate or facilitate our journey to Futureville.

# THREE
# EVOLUTION

## THE ENLIGHTENMENT

Where's my flying car? When I was nine years old, a popular movie put in my mind the idea that I would have a flying car by 2015. You may recall the final scene from *Back to the Future* when Doc Brown returns from the year 2015 to warn Marty McFly and his girlfriend about their future family. They jump into the DeLorean time machine; Marty says they don't have enough road to accelerate to eighty-eight miles per hour—the speed necessary for time travel; Doc responds, "Roads? Where we're going, we don't need roads"; and the car takes to the sky. Well, I remember the scene, and I'm still waiting for my flying car. Sure, we have cars with navigation systems (à la James Bond), and cars with voice recognition (à la *Knight Rider*), and some cars will even parallel park themselves (à la *Herbie, the Love Bug*), but when are they going to fly?

Maybe you're not as enamored with airborne automobiles as I am, but there is likely something about the future that captured your imagination as a child—something amazing you expected to have or do by now. Travel to outer space? Own a robot butler? Play holographic chess with a Wookie? We didn't just carry these expectations because we were impressionable children. We were born into a world that convinced us progress was inevitable. We were told that whatever we have today will be replaced by an even better version tomorrow. Consider how rapidly the world evolved. The time between inventing powered flight and landing a man on the moon was the span of a single life (seventy-six years). And if the Ford Model T in 1908 could evolve into the Ford Taurus by 1985, then is a flying Ford by 2015 really expecting too much? I don't think so.

We may still be driving with wheels on the ground, but that doesn't detract from the incredible advancements in the last thirty years. Progress in communications and computers has fundamentally transformed our lives, and advances in medicine have not just transformed our lives but saved them. A century ago the leading cause of death in the United States was the flu, and the average life expectancy for men was forty-six years.[1] We do live in an age of remarkable progress, and we should thank God for that, but the widely held belief in progress has also come to shape the way many Christians think about the future.

In the last chapter we entered the Perisphere to get a peek at the culmination of the Christian narrative. We explored the Bible's description of a coming age where order, beauty, and abundance reach full maturity and where all evil is eradicated—a world represented by Futureville, the garden city of God. But questions remain: How will this world of tomorrow be achieved? What pathway has God ordained to make his world one saturated with shalom? For many modern Christians, the pathway to Futureville is believed to be one of continuous progress.

We can trace this path back to a day in 1666 when Sir Isaac Newton was contemplating the universe under a tree in his garden. He observed an apple fall to the ground and was inspired to define the law of gravity. In time, Newton observed and defined numerous other natural laws that led Western civilization to construct a different model of the universe. Scientific method rather than superstition would come to shape the culture, and with it the modern era was born.

The discoveries of Newton, along with other minds of the Enlightenment, began the evolution of progress that we still find ourselves in today. Early mechanical physics produced the steam engine, which launched the Industrial Revolution. Cities grew, economies expanded, and new frontiers were explored for raw materials. Eventually, industry produced devices to harness electricity, unlock the secrets of living cells, and even tap the power of the atom. The Enlightenment also brought revolutions in the social sphere. Progressive thought toppled monarchies in Europe, and a bold, new democratic experiment was launched in the New World—a republic founded on Enlightenment principles called the United States of America.

The pace of scientific and social change was so rapid during this time that many people came to believe that tomorrow was destined to be better than today. This was an uncommon belief in the premodern world, which viewed the cosmos as static or driven by endlessly repeating historical cycles. The new idea of progress kindled the imaginations of modern minds like British philosopher Francis Bacon. His 1627 book *New Atlantis* described a utopian future marked by reason and science, and a civilization transformed by inventions. Bacon envisioned superfoods and superdrinks providing longevity and superhuman strength, robot servants, flying machines, and new animal species created by scientists. He dismissed premodern ideas of heavenly salvation in favor of an earth perfected through human achievement. Bacon's *New Atlantis* was a secular vision of the future with scientists in the role of priests tending a temple of human knowledge.

This Enlightenment belief in progress gained even more momentum with the publication of a bold, new theory by Charles Darwin in 1859. *The Origin of Species* popularized the notion that life evolved from simple organisms into the diverse and complex creatures now occupying the planet. The theory of evolution gave scientific legitimacy to a belief in perpetual progress. If bacteria became jellyfish, and jellyfish became minnows, and minnows became mice, and mice became monkeys, and monkeys became men, then sometime in the future men would become . . . supermen! Continual progress, evolution taught, was inherent to the universe.

As these new ideas began to intersect Christianity, which by any measure had its origin in the premodern world, the impact was explosive. Traditional religion was challenged by a new worldview predicated on natural law and science. Debates raged about the authority and accuracy of the Bible, science fueled a surge in antisupernaturalism, and foundational doctrines of the faith came into question. While important, these controversies are beyond the scope of this book. My focus here is on how modernity's belief in progress influenced Christians' views of the future and their search for significance in the present.

By the nineteenth century, the Enlightenment had lifted Europe, and European Christianity, to the height of global power. Western states colonized much of the world, and the modern missionary movement began to carry the Christian faith to every corner of the globe. This era of colonialism, together with advances occurring in every area of life and industry, led many Western Christians to believe that the world would continue to evolve until it reflected the full glory of the garden city of God. They believed in time the whole planet would be perfected through Christian faith and advances in civilization. Once this perfection was achieved, Christ would then return to reign upon the earth and fulfill the vision of Futureville.[2]

When a Christian vision of the future is mingled with modernity's belief in perpetual progress, it results in a path to Futureville based on continuity. In other words, it believes there is an uninterrupted progression from the world we currently occupy (marked by chaos, ugliness, and scarcity) to the world of the future (marked by order, beauty, and abundance). The wilderness of this world will evolve into the garden city, but we are not passive in this evolution. As Francis Bacon advocated four hundred years ago, humanity has the responsibility to create the world of tomorrow through its own intelligence and ingenuity. While the world may develop slowly through evolution, we are to be agents of revolution who bring change with intentionality and with accelerating speed. As President Kennedy famously said, "Our problems are man-made, therefore they can be solved by man."[3] A more modern statement has never been spoken.

The belief that we are responsible for creating Futureville fueled many ministries and Christian initiatives. Christians who promoted the abolition of slavery, women's rights, prison reform, health care, education, and fair labor laws were in many cases motivated by this progressive pathway. They believed it was their duty to create a society that adhered closely to the ethics of Christian faith as a way of transforming the world into God's kingdom. William Wilberforce (1759–1833), perhaps the most celebrated social reformer in English history, held this belief. He called "the suppression of the slave trade" one of two "great objectives" of his life that God Almighty had set before him.[4] It took him decades and great personal sacrifice, but eventually he succeeded in passing a bill in Parliament to end the slave trade. Wilberforce saw the social reforms pursued by

Christians as instrumental in creating the shalom-filled world envisioned by the narrative of Scripture.

I trust you can already sense how appealing the path of social evolution is to many Christians. A belief in perpetual progress is certainly a hope-filled vision of tomorrow, and for those eager for a life of meaning and significance, the call to reshape the world into the garden city of God definitely fills that need. But faith in this path to Futureville would not go unchallenged.

## THE CAROUSEL

H. G. Wells is best known for his science fiction novels *The Time Machine* (1895) and *The War of the Worlds* (1898), but he was also a thoroughly modern mind and an influential futurist who wrote extensively about the glorious destiny that awaited humanity. Shaped by his belief in evolution and progress, Wells concluded a lecture in 1902 with this optimistic declaration:

> Everything seems pointing to the belief that we are entering upon a progress that will go on with an ever widening and an ever more confident stride, for ever. . . . If we care to look, we can foresee growing knowledge, growing order, and presently a deliberate improvement of the blood and character of the race.[5]

However, twenty-five years later, Wells's optimism had faltered. In his book *Mind at the End of Its Tether*, Wells spoke of a more ominous tomorrow:

> A tremendous series of events has forced upon the intelligent observer the realization that the human story has already come to an end and that Homo sapiens, as he has been pleased to call himself, is in his present form played out.[6]

What occurred to dismantle Wells's belief in eternal progress? World War I. The "Great War" left Europe in ruins and 37 million people dead. The same forces that had led people to believe in progress—scientific advances and European imperialism—had been used to inflict unprecedented devastation upon the earth. Science had given the world electricity, but it had also produced chemical weapons. Colonialism was carrying Western civilization to the ends of the earth, but it also ignited conflict between empires on a scale never before seen. World War I still ranks as one of the deadliest conflicts in human history, and it utterly shattered Europe's belief in progress.

The same was not true on the other side of the Atlantic. The United States entered the war relatively late. Americans accounted for only 2 percent of Allied casualties, and most of its citizens were far removed from the destruction experienced in Europe. Walt Disney, for example, served as a Red Cross ambulance driver, but he did not arrive in France until November 1918—the same month the war officially ended. In the aftermath of the war, European power began to diminish and empires crumbled, but American strength began to expand and its fortunes rose. Just as many Europeans were abandoning a belief in progress, Americans were embracing it.

Disney was one of them. He returned from Europe still believing in a "Great Big Beautiful Tomorrow"—the theme song to what would become one of his most passionate projects. Half a century later, Disney's optimism was on full display at the 1964 New York World's Fair, where he created his Carousel of Progress that took visitors on a journey through the advances experienced by a typical American family over one hundred years and forecasted even better days ahead.[7]

I don't know if Walt Disney ever saw the irony of his attraction's name, but it captures the paradox at the heart of evolution's path to Futureville. Progress assumes linear advancement. Technology, society, and quality of life are destined to improve over time. A carousel, on the other hand, is designed to repeat its course in endless cycles. What goes around comes around, which is hardly progress.

This progress paradox is what left H. G. Wells and many other modern people so disillusioned. By the twentieth century, progress was happening in many areas, and great improvement was evident in the lives of millions, but the most basic deficiencies within the human race proved frustratingly resistant to change. Greed, prejudice, fear, and envy could not be removed from the population as easily as polio or poverty, and these maladies manifested themselves in the most horrible ways during two world wars, genocides, the Cold War, and the new threat of nuclear holocaust. While the past century was one of unparalleled technological progress, it was also the most violent. One study estimates that 200 million people died in armed conflict between 1900 and 2000.[8] Human exploitation has fared no better. Wilberforce may have ended the British involvement in the slave trade in 1807, but today there remain 27 million slaves in the world—more than at any time in history.[9]

These facts make the promise of inevitable evolution toward a glorious future seem difficult to accept. Modernity has shown that we can improve society beyond its static and dark experience in the Middle Ages, but our ability to create Futureville through our own will and ingenuity is another matter. It seems the more things have evolved, the more obvious our sinful natures have become. The brutality and injustice we assign to past ages are no less potent in our technological times; we've simply become more sophisticated about them. "History doesn't repeat itself," someone once said, "but it does rhyme." This is why the path of evolution cannot offer us an enduring hope. Progress is real, but so are the endless cycles of human cruelty and injustice that stain our world.

## THE CRUSADERS

Following the progress-shattering events of the twentieth century, fewer Christians believe the world is continuously evolving toward perfection, but many Christians still believe their purpose is to change the world. As noted earlier, historically it was Christians in the West who pioneered advances in education, health care, and human rights. Many of the just and compassionate social values we take for granted today were cultivated by Christian activists in earlier times. Like the advances in science and technology that brought good into our world, social activism is a value worth celebrating; but it too carries a hidden danger—especially for my generation, which finds this call particularly appealing.

Consider the research done by Andy Crouch. He hypothesized that interest in having a global impact was on the rise among the young, so he searched the Harvard University library database for book titles containing various forms of the phrase *change the world*. The number of books with the phrase in the title published between 2000 and 2010 was more than double the number published in the 1990s, and five times more than all books published between 1900 and 1989.[10] It seems everyone wants to "change the world," but for many Christians this call has been decoupled from an optimistic view of history. In a strange twist, a great deal of Christian social engagement is now driven by pessimism rather than optimism, and World War I also played a role in this shift.

Studying the changing views of Christians in that era, George Marsden wrote:

> World War I had produced among many conservative evangelicals both a sense of crisis over the revolution in morals and a renewed concern for the welfare of civilization. . . . German civilization during the war was portrayed as the essence of barbarism, despite its strongly Christian heritage. Could the same thing happen here? The strong winds of change suggested that it could.[11]

Many Christians no longer wanted to transform society because they hoped to evolve toward the garden city of God; they did it because they feared devolving into a culture dominated by unchristian values.

James Davidson Hunter, author of *To Change the World: The Irony, Tragedy, and Possibility of Christianity in the Late Modern World*, describes current efforts to transform society this way:

> The rhetoric of world changing originates from a profound angst that the world is changing for the worse, and that we must act urgently. There's a sense of panic that things are falling apart. If we don't respond now, we'll lose the things we cherish the most. What animates this talk is a desperation to hold on to something when the world no longer makes sense.[12]

Whether we are talking about the current fear of regress or the earlier belief in progress, one element of this pathway to Futureville has remained unchanged: those who pursue and accomplish social change are exalted. If you want your life to matter, if you are seeking meaning and purpose in the present, then you must devote yourself to changing the world for Christ. Despite the historical baggage, I refer to those carrying this view as "crusaders." They find their significance in pursuit of a divine mission to transform the world. These crusaders and the change they accomplish are often worth celebrating. Can you imagine a world deprived of the influence of William

Wilberforce, Elizabeth Cady Stanton, or Martin Luther King Jr.? Christian activists often have prophetic and transformative roles in society, but what about everyone else?

How does a dentist, roofer, or homemaker find meaning and purpose? Does pulling a tooth, fixing a roof, or changing a diaper really matter if the Christian's purpose is social transformation? How might these followers of Christ find significance? Are they required to give their surplus time and energy to "the cause"—whatever it may be? Or is real meaning only to be found by abandoning those callings to become crusaders pursuing something that really matters? When the goal of Christianity is evolving society (or preventing its devolving), real value is reserved for those who make a measurable and lasting impact on the world. This fact can put a heavy burden on those seeking lives of significance or utterly discourage those unable to give more of their time and treasure to Christian cultural causes.

As the call to change the world has risen in volume in recent years, it's been fascinating to see the effect among peers within my own vocation. I have seen friends enter pastoral ministry with a desire to make a difference and then leave ministry for the same reason. Some have concluded that the church no longer carries enough cultural influence to catalyze change, so they exit the pastorate to enter a business, a nonprofit organization, or in one case a government role looking for a career that will really impact the world. Fifteen years ago, when I first started attending pastoral gatherings, the banter was often about preaching techniques or a new teaching curriculum. Sometimes they ventured into talks about launching new worship services or planting a new congregation. Messages about politics or social issues were nonexistent. Not anymore. Ministry conferences today are likely to give as much airtime to poverty, sex trafficking, or environmental care as they are to church growth. It used to be the megachurch pastor who was most celebrated, but that distinction now goes to the urban pastor with a half dozen affiliated NGOs to his name. The key question is no longer, "How big is your church?" but, "How big is your impact?"

To a large degree I welcome and celebrate this shift. We do need to be thinking outside the walls of the church, but we still must recognize that within this form of Christianity not everyone carries value. Not everyone's work is validated. The woman organizing the voter registration drive? Yes. The woman teaching sixth graders how to sing in harmony? No. The man leading a nonprofit organization to rescue prostitutes from the street? Yes. The man leading a for-profit business to repair cars? No. The minister organizing a boycott of a corporation using child labor overseas? Yes. The minister listening to and praying for patients at the local hospital? No.

Like Francis Bacon's *New Atlantis* where the priests of science were the most celebrated, Christian communities dedicated to evolution also have a hierarchy of importance with social crusaders at the top of the heap. For everyone else, purpose remains elusive. It may be glimpsed in volunteer efforts in support of a greater cause, but it cannot be grasped in one's ordinary existence. So for the majority of Christians, the path of evolution does not offer a life of dignity and significance because their work in this world does not bring lasting change and therefore does not ultimately matter. Real value and dignity are reserved for those on the front lines of the cultural crusades.

## THE BATTLEFIELD

Where does the path of evolution ultimately lead us? If we venture all the way along this road to Futureville, what will we discover? Will we find the garden city we long for—a renewed world of order, beauty, and abundance? Will we find ourselves in the present wilderness of the world with no signs of real transformation? Unfortunately, rather than a garden or even a wilderness, the path of social evolution leads to a war-torn battlefield.

When we believe it is our responsibility to reshape society to create the world of tomorrow, the obvious question becomes, which tomorrow? The future I want or the future you want? Invariably the desire to create and control the future leads to conflict as individuals and tribes fight to impose their own visions of tomorrow upon others. Colonialism, as already mentioned, was a world-changing part of modernity. European states took possession of other nations with the goal of imposing their vision and values upon occupied peoples. The conflicts that resulted and their aftereffects still reverberate through the world today.

This quality of evolution's path also requires us to label others as either allies or enemies of our mission to impact the world. Consider Jerry Falwell's infamous words following the terrorist attacks on 9/11: "I really believe that the pagans, and the abortionists, and the feminists, and the gays and the lesbians who are actively trying to make that an alternative lifestyle, the ACLU, People for the American Way—all of them who have tried to secularize America—I point the finger in their face and say, 'you helped this happen.'"[13]

As the leader of the Moral Majority, Falwell had been crusading for decades to shape America into a country that more closely reflected his Christian values. Those seeking a more secular future, therefore, were categorized as enemies and obstacles to the future he believed God had ordained. This sort of rhetoric, no matter what side of the culture wars it's coming from, does not lead us closer to Futureville. It does not cultivate shalom. Instead, it ferments more fear, anger, and strife; it transforms the already threatening wilderness of the world into a lethal, winner-take-all battlefield in which every person's value is determined by his or her support or obstruction of the desired future I am trying to build.

The bitter fruit of this path was made obvious to me during a meeting near Washington, DC, a few years ago. I was invited to participate in two days of talks between conservative religious leaders and national advocates of gay rights. Unlike me, most of the people in the room had spent years fighting one another over legalizing same-sex marriage. One side envisioned a future with a traditional definition of family (husband, wife, and children); the other sought to expand the legal protections of marriage to include same-sex couples. The anger and wounds displayed by both sides at the off-the-record gathering were not merely a result of holding different convictions on a complicated issue. The worst damage was the result of seeing the other group as the barrier to creating the "right" future for the country. It was never said explicitly, but the message was clear: *the future of our society would be brighter if you were not a part of it.*

Most of those at the meeting did not use the time to express their views or to convince others of their position's moral superiority. Instead, many expressed the pain and bitterness of being labeled by the opposing camp. Words like *bigot*, *ungodly*, *depraved*, and *homophobic* were mentioned as leaving deep and lasting wounds by both sides. Decades of anger and scars came out into the open, sometimes accompanied by tears. The name-calling and dismissive labels used by each side were deemed justifiable because those on the other side were the "enemy"; they were to be defeated with overwhelming political, cultural, and economic force to achieve a "greater good." After all, if the other side won, progress (however each side defined it) would be lost.

What both sides of the culture war forget is that when we label another person or group as the "enemy" because they oppose our vision of the future, we also reduce their value. We diminish, at least in our eyes, some of their God-given worth by viewing them as objects to be removed rather than people to be loved. Whenever we diminish the value of people created in God's image, we cannot be moving closer to shalom; we cannot be drawing closer to Futureville.

Adding to the battlefield is the use of worldly force and coercion to accomplish the goal of social transformation. Simply put, the path of evolution creates bullies. If shaping and controlling the future is our mission, we are tempted to believe that if we control the levers of power in Washington, in Hollywood, on Wall Street, then we can steer the culture in the direction God wants, and wouldn't God rather have us in control of these levers than our enemies? With more power, we tell ourselves, we can muscle our agenda into existence and force others to submit to our vision of the future. When we believe our vision is right, or when we believe it is God-given, we never call our tactics "bullying." Bullies are bad people, after all, and we have the best of intentions. Of course Hitler, Stalin, Mao, and Pol Pot were also trying to create perfect societies. From their perspectives and those of their followers, they also had good intentions. This is why the road to hell, as the saying goes, is paved with them.

None of this means power cannot be used for good. Humble and godly leaders like Wilberforce have shown that shalom can be cultivated when power is in the hands of Christ's servants. But often power, particularly when used to silence one's opponents, can result in unintentional damage. Using worldly devices to bring about a more godly future was the tactic pursued by Falwell's Moral Majority. The group became a key player within the Republican Party in the 1970s and '80s, and many believe its influence continued to be felt well into the twenty-first century. But Ed Dobson, one of Falwell's deputies, has a more sober assessment of its effect:

> Did the Moral Majority really make a difference? During the height of the Moral Majority, we were taking in millions of dollars a year. We published a magazine, organized state chapters, lobbied Congress, aired a radio program, and more. Did it work? Is the moral condition of America better because of our efforts? Even a casual observation of the current moral climate suggests that despite all the time, money, and energy—despite the political power—we failed. Things have not gotten better, they have gotten worse.[14]

What Dobson and other Christian cultural crusaders have learned is that you can win a battle but still lose the war. Consider that after thirty years of partisan Christian activism in the United States, young people have come to view Christians not as a hope-filled people of love and charity, but as homophobic, hypocritical, and hyperpolitical.[15] And rather than transforming America into a more God-fearing nation, research conducted by David Campbell and Robert Putnam found a direct correlation between the rise in secularism among young adults and the political crusades of conservative Christians.[16] People born since the 1980s in the United States have only known a politicized church; they've only seen Christian crusaders in the public square carrying the belligerent values of progress—and they are not impressed.

The path of evolution has its roots in modern thinking, a belief in the perpetual advancement of civilization and the human race. It invites us to join a revolution to make Futureville a reality. But progress has turned out to be a false hope. Rather than unending evolution, history has shown we are incapable of changing the qualities that have always haunted our sinful natures. And rather than offering meaning and purpose to all, this path only celebrates the cultural crusaders who noticeably change the world. Most of us are confined to lives of relative worthlessness as we engage in lesser callings.

Perhaps most disheartening, walking the path of evolution makes the world into a more dangerous and fractured place, a battlefield with each tribe fighting for its own vision of tomorrow. Over the last century, this path to Futureville has revealed its shortcomings. Unfortunately, the alternative path chosen by many Christians has fared no better.

# FOUR
# EVACUATION

## THE SHIPWRECK

The goal of any warning is to provoke action, but not all warnings carry the same urgency. For example, when the Check Engine light appears on my dashboard, I know addressing it can easily wait a few days or even a week. Similarly, my public library kindly sends a warning notice when my borrowed books are nearly overdue, but I often have at least five days before any fine is levied. When my four-year-old daughter warns that she has to go to the bathroom, however, she does not mean, "I'm a little uncomfortable. Could you find a bathroom soon?" What Lucy means is, "I'm going to defecate in my pants in five . . . four . . . three . . ." Her warning carries the highest urgency. All other tasks are put aside as we scan for the nearest restroom and move her a safe distance away from innocent bystanders.

The Bible includes warnings about God's final judgment of the world and the calamities that accompany it. During some periods of history the warnings were largely ignored or mythologized to the point of dismissal. Yet for many Christians today these warnings carry the highest urgency. Popular books and sermons about the end times are surrounded by images of flames and destruction, and their messages can often be summarized by simple, frightening imperatives: Be prepared! Save yourself! Repent! One description of the future I heard repeatedly as a younger Christian presented the world as full of blindfolded people walking toward a cliff. "They are heading toward destruction," the speaker would press upon the audience, "unless you intervene!" This grabs your attention and calls for an immediate response.

These alarming warnings about the future stand in contrast to the message of evolution. If you recall, the path of evolution affirmed the gradual improvement of the world through human agency. That road to Futureville said our task was not to rescue souls from destruction but to improve the world through reason and ingenuity. It was a gradual march to a glorious tomorrow. But in the early twentieth century, when Western civilization began questioning its belief in perpetual progress, Christians increasingly abandoned this vision. They came to believe the world was deteriorating into moral and spiritual chaos and thereby provoking the judgment of God. The end was near, as so many sandwich-board-wearing street evangelists warned, and our only job was to repent and be saved. This is the simple vision behind the second pathway to Futureville—evacuation.

This more alarming road is displayed in a parable written by Rev. Dr. Theodore O. Wedel in 1953 that has found its way into the unofficial canon of American Christianity. Seeking to illustrate the tendency of the church to drift from its mission, Dr. Wedel compared it to a lifesaving station on a treacherous coastline where shipwrecks were common. "The building was just a hut, and there was only one boat," he wrote, "but the few devoted members kept a constant watch over the sea, and with no thought for themselves, went out day and night tirelessly searching for the lost."[1] We will explore the central message of Dr. Wedel's parable later, but first we must see what his metaphor implies about the nature of the world. If we view the church as a lifesaving station, we must see the world as a sinking ship and its inhabitants as doomed passengers.

While Christians adhering to this vision may affirm the world's original beauty and goodness, they now see it as a lost cause akin to the *Titanic* after striking the iceberg. No amount of human effort is going to keep the world afloat; its destiny is sealed. They believe the world will be utterly destroyed and abandoned by God. If you recall, evolution believed there is continuity between this world and the next. It said the present world will gradually become the garden city of God. Evacuation, by contrast, is predicated on discontinuity—the view that nothing from the present world will endure apart from the souls of those rescued from destruction. Everything God created in the beginning will be destroyed and replaced with an entirely new and perfected creation. According to this path, God will press a Reset button on the universe and reboot creation. The old, worn-out world will be thrown away and replaced with a brand-new one. In this scenario Futureville is reached by abandoning this world like passengers on a sinking ship.

## THE ESCAPE

Over the last century this ominous pathway to the future has come to dominate much of American evangelicalism and the way many Christians relate to the world. If the world is to be utterly destroyed, separation is the only logical response. Escape the sinking ship, or sink with it.

The path of evacuation seems to lack all the hope and optimism that made evolution so attractive. So why do so many Christians find this message of doom appealing? There are many personal and societal factors, but one of the most powerful is the promise of safety. Central to evacuation is the belief that believers will be entirely spared from the pain and suffering awaiting the rest of humanity. Before any judgment is poured out upon the earth, those who belong to Christ will be removed from the planet in an event popularly known as the Rapture. Once his people are safely removed, God may then proceed to judge and destroy the earth. While evacuation theology emphasizes the decline and destruction of the world, there remains a narrow hope. It is the hope of escape.

The appeal of this path to Futureville, however, goes

beyond the hope of escape. We cannot separate the rising popularity of this view from the reality of evolution's failure. As noted in the previous chapter, the promise of perpetual progress was found empty in the wake of World War I, and the horrible conflicts that marked the twentieth century, including World War II, convinced many Christians that the world was becoming worse rather than better. Two additional factors added credibility to evacuation's path to the future. First, the establishment of the modern state of Israel in 1948 was seized upon by adherents of a particular system of biblical interpretation that emphasized evacuation as proof that they were living in the last days.[2] Second, the development of nuclear weapons and the subsequent Cold War fueled nightmares about global annihilation. For the first time in history the destruction of all life on earth was not only humanly imaginable but also achievable. Given our species' spotty track record with technology, it seemed inevitable that we would use this new power to destroy the planet sooner rather than later.

These unprecedented realities caused many Christians to believe that the end was indeed near and that this world was on the edge of destruction—by nuclear holocaust, God's wrath, or both. This message was popularized in the best-selling book *The Late Great Planet Earth* by Hal Lindsey. Lindsey connected biblical prophecy with current events and concluded that Judgment Day was drawing near. While certainly not the first voice to offer such a prediction, the timing of Lindsey's book at the height of the Cold War triggered huge sales and launched an entire Armageddon industry. Books, films, radio shows, and ministries about the end of days proliferated in the 1970s and '80s. A generation of Christians became convinced they would be the last to occupy the earth. By 1993, a national poll found that 20 percent of Americans believed the second coming of Christ would happen near the year 2000.[3]

The hope of escaping the pain and suffering prophesied for the end of days motivated many Christians to disconnect from the world around them. Why bother with art, government, the environment, science, or social ills if the earth will soon be destroyed and replaced? Devoting energy to such things is akin to rearranging deck chairs on the *Titanic*. As a result, many white Christians remained disengaged from the social crusades of the twentieth century.[4] This mind-set is what led Oliver Wendell Holmes to comment, "Some people are so heavenly minded that they are no earthly good."[5] This attitude persisted in much of the American church until the legalization of abortion in 1973, when a new generation of cultural crusaders was mustered—a trend discussed in the previous chapter. Nonetheless, even these crusaders found it incredibly difficult to mobilize Christians for social action who adhered to an evacuation theology.

The accusation that Christians who are committed to evacuation are "no earthly good" may be too severe. While they do eagerly await their final rescue at the Rapture, some have been thoughtful enough to prepare those who will be left behind. One evacuationist, for example, has created "The Post Rapture Survival Guide," with materials for those unfortunate souls not prepared for the end of days. He wrote:

> Let me be real frank with you. If you are reading this manual and the rapture has already occurred, then you probably are not going to physically survive; you most likely will die. This manual is about the survival of your soul. You are going to go through terrible suffering. The only question is whether you will go to Heaven or go to hell when you die.[6]

The writer captures the essence of the evacuation theology belief in the Rapture and its link to discontinuity. He's focused on his own escape and the "survival of your soul," but nothing else.

## THE CLERGY

Every vision of the future determines how we relate to the world by giving us hope and purpose. The path of evolution's hope is found in our human ability to improve the world, and our purpose is to transform the earth into Futureville. Evacuation, as we have already seen, finds hope in escape. The world will be destroyed, and one's only hope is being snatched away by God before the hammer falls. This vision of escape also determines our sense of purpose. If nothing of this world will endure apart from the souls of the redeemed, then the only work that can carry any significance is rescuing souls. For this reason the most celebrated people on this path are those dedicating their full-time energy to rescuing the lost. If you really want your life to matter, the path of evacuation says, ministry is the only work that can offer eternal satisfaction.

In many Christian communities adhering to the evacuation

pathway, there is an implicit—and sometimes explicit—hierarchy of value based on each person's work. At the top are cross-cultural missionaries. They have given themselves fully to the task of rescuing souls and have embraced the challenge of doing this in a foreign setting, often at great personal risk and discomfort. Below them on the ladder are pastors who serve full-time in the church to save the lost and build up the redeemed at home. If you are not a pastor or missionary, you may still be able to scratch together some semblance of value by using your extra time and money to support their work. As I have heard many times, every Christian must either "go, give, or pray." If you do not go into ministry yourself, then at least support the work by giving money and praying for those who are doing the work you are not.

The single-minded emphasis upon rescuing souls communicates to the majority of Christians that their work in the world does not matter. Whether you are a teacher, dentist, artist, or mechanic is irrelevant to God and his kingdom. The tasks that occupy most of your time, and therefore most of your life, cannot matter if the entire world is going to burn. At best you may behave like a pastor or missionary amid your labor. Share your faith with a coworker. Invite her to church. Start a lunch-hour Bible study in the office. Give more of your salary to mission work. Occasionally some affirmation may come by applying your profession within a Christian organization. Being an accountant at the local bank may not matter, but being an accountant for a local Christian ministry brings you one step closer to doing real "kingdom work."

A pastor in Boston recounted the story of a woman in his congregation who was a lawyer for the Environmental Protection Agency. She played a vital role in the cleanup of Boston Harbor—one of the most polluted waterways in the country—but the pastor said, "The only time we have ever recognized her in church was for her role in teaching second-grade Sunday school. And of course we absolutely should celebrate Sunday school teachers, but why did we never celebrate her incredible contribution to our whole city as a Christian, taking care of God's creation?"[7]

The reason may be the influence of evacuation theology. We have been shaped for more than a century by the assumption that God cares about one thing—saving souls. If we believe the church is a lifesaving station and the world is a sinking ship, then it makes sense to focus with laser precision on those doing the rescuing. The urgency of the task demands no less. In order to keep Christians focused on the most important work, we have pushed aside anything that might distract from it—including the cleanup of Boston Harbor. If all the world's a stage, to use Shakespeare's metaphor, there may be many actors with many different roles, but the spotlight must remain on the clergy. Of course, for those of us standing in the spotlight, it is difficult to see anyone else.

One of the reasons for keeping the spotlight on ministry is to attract more people into this all-important work. There is no question this strategy is effective, but it carries a hidden danger. When the evacuation path celebrates clergy, and those who behave like them, it has the effect of attracting some people into ministry for the wrong reasons. They may pursue a ministry role not because they are genuinely gifted or called but because they are seeking significance. They are drawn to the spotlight with the promise that in its glow their lives will really matter.

You may be asking, what is the harm of recruiting more missionaries and pastors? Shouldn't we be encouraged that the message of the gospel is spreading and more people are coming to faith in Christ? Didn't Jesus say, "The harvest is plentiful, but the laborers are few"?[8] Yes, it is a wonderful thing to see the message of Christ go forth, and we will discuss the importance of reconciliation to God through Christ in chapter 7. We should also remember the apostle Paul's instructions to honor our leaders in the church who teach us the mysteries of God.[9] Still, these truths do not eliminate the danger posed by evacuation's narrow view of purpose.

First, as mentioned above, when only clergy are honored in our communities, some become attracted to the role from a desire for significance. This may in part explain the extraordinarily high rates of pastoral burnout, addiction, physical ailments, family breakdown, and depression.[10] They simply were never meant to be ministers, but their churches, communities, and even families convinced them to pursue ministry as a way of securing significance. Bill was the first person in his family to attend college. Given the family's strong Christian heritage, it was assumed that with his higher education he would become a pastor. Four decades later he tearfully explained to me how his parents still express disappointment over his decision not to enter ministry. I know parents and grandparents who pray every day that at least one of their children will become a full-time Christian worker, and they regularly tell their children about this desire. They are sending them a clear message: *Of course we will always love you, but if you enter ministry we'll be especially proud (and so will God).* I have had teenagers in my church ask why they should bother going to college. "Why shouldn't I just go overseas and help on the mission field instead?" one asked.

Second, celebrating only clergy devalues every one of God's children who is not called to full-time ministry. Their work, and therefore the majority of their lives, are dismissed as wasted on temporal things rather than invested in eternal treasures. G. K. Chesterton once said, "Everyone on this earth should believe, amid whatever madness or moral failure, that his life and temperament have some object on the earth. Everyone on the earth should believe that he has something to give to the world which cannot otherwise be given."[11] The path of evacuation dismisses this belief as it makes those in the kingdom of God committed to non-ministry vocations feel like second-class citizens who must strive for a meaningful existence by contributing more of their free time and extra resources to saving souls because their primary calling carries no enduring value.

For young adults today, most of whom are delaying marriage and family much longer and therefore find identity in their work, the contemporary church organized around the assumption of the nuclear family has little to say apart from, "Come join our soul-saving work." While prior generations may have found this message of escape and safety attractive, for a generation that is desperately seeking significance, the path of evacuation offers it only to the select few—the clergy. All others are condemned to an earthly existence devoid of real purpose. Is it any wonder why so many young people are abandoning the church in search of a life that offers meaning in this world and not just in the world to come?

## THE ISLANDS

We have seen how evacuation finds hope through separating and escaping from the world, and how purpose is reserved for those engaged in this effort. Today, however, few observers of American Christianity would conclude the church is "so heavenly minded that it is no earthly good." With a 4.63 billion dollar annual Christian book and merchandise industry—not to mention Christian films, radio, and entertainment—many believe the church is worldlier than ever. How did a movement predicated on escaping the world come to look so much like it?[12] Dietrich Bonhoeffer understood the inherent danger of the evacuation path. He observed, "Any attempt to escape from the world must sooner or later be paid for with a sinful surrender to the world."[13]

Christian fundamentalists in the early twentieth century sought safe separation by prohibiting listening to popular music, dancing, watching movies, playing cards, smoking, drinking alcohol, and other "worldly" pursuits. Presumably these vices were evidence of the world's decline into depravity. Few Christians now believe a rogue game of Crazy Eights will hasten holy judgment, but the mind-set behind such prohibitions is still present. Today the list of offenses has changed and become more politically focused, with sexuality often getting the most attention. This fact was on display in 2012 when a Christian business leader created a controversy when asked about his company's financial support of groups opposed to same-sex marriage. He said, "I think we are inviting God's judgment on our nation when we shake our fist at him and say, 'We know better than you as to what constitutes a marriage.'"[14] Issues like homosexuality, abortion, feminism, and liberal politics in general are to be avoided by Christians, this perspective says, and if the rest of America knew what was best it would avoid them as well. These remarks correspond to the Christian response to society outlined in the previous chapter, where we discussed how cultural crusaders seek to slow or reverse the unrighteous devolution of society.

But when the goal of cultural revolution fails, as it often does, the faithful turn to a backup plan—separation. This is where the way of evacuation fits. The goal of separation is to protect yourself and those you love from the dangerous world that is "slouching towards Gomorrah," as the former nominee to the U.S. Supreme Court Robert Bork said of America in his book *Slouching Towards Gomorrah*. He wrote:

> The best strategy for those of us who detest modern liberalism and all its works may be simply to seek sanctuary, to attempt to create small islands of decency and civility in the midst of a subpagan culture. Gated communities and

the home-schooling movement are the beginning of such responses.[15]

In fact, the formation of "islands of decency" began well before Bork penned these words. When popular youth culture emerged in the 1950s followed by the social upheaval of the 1960s, many Christians feared for their children and teens. How could they be protected from the ungodly influences of sex, drugs, and rock and roll? Youth ministries emerged to offer Christian teens a safe, fun alternative while insulating them from the sins of the world outside the church, but the creation of a safe, Christian youth culture had an unintended consequence.

When these teens reached adulthood in the 1970s and '80s, they brought their desire for a safe, Christian subculture that paralleled the popular culture with them. "Why should the pagans have all the good music?" was a motto that captured the values of baby-boomer Christians at the time. What emerged was a massive, and profitable, Christian marketplace offering virtually everything the secular culture could—but imprinted with a Jesus logo. Apart from the exponential growth in Christian media and entertainment since the 1970s, we have also seen Jesus-branded knockoffs of secular trends from diet programs and breath mints, to apparel and poker chips.

The exaltation of clergy and the demotion of other vocations also contributed to the creation of a parallel evangelical subculture. Christians employed in secular professions found little or no affirmation of their work from the church, so some sought a more God-honoring outlet for their skills by adding a Christian veneer. They created Christian art, opened Christian businesses, and launched Christian music labels and Christian schools. Today it is possible for a believer to wear Christian clothes on a Christian cruise vacation, where she mingles with Christian pop artists, purchases best-selling Christian books, catches a Christian movie in the theater, and uploads her vacation videos to a Christian version of YouTube for her Christian friends to watch at her Christian college. We have created a self-contained Christian facsimile of the world.

How did a form of Christianity predicated on urgently escaping a doomed world become so worldly? To answer that question we must return to Reverend Wedel's 1953 lifesaving station analogy. In his story the lifesaving station had a simple, narrow mission: to rescue souls. Frequent storm warnings kept the station on alert and focused, but when warnings became less urgent, or when fewer shipwrecks occurred, the lifesaving station drifted from its mission. He wrote:

> Some of the members of the life-saving station were unhappy that the building was so crude and poorly equipped. They felt that a more comfortable place should be provided as the first refuge of those saved from the sea. They replaced the emergency cots with beds and put better furniture in the enlarged building. Now the life-saving station became a popular gathering place for its members, and they decorated it beautifully because they used it as a sort of club.[16]

Eventually, Wedel said, the station became so inwardly focused on its own comfort that it was no longer equipped to save lives. His parable concluded, "If you visit that sea coast today, you will find a number of exclusive clubs along the shore. Shipwrecks are frequent in those waters, but most of the people drown."[17]

The goal of Wedel's story was to prevent the church from drifting from its single purpose, but a half century after his parable was written, his warning now appears prophetic. The rampant consumerism in the church and its inward drive to ensure its members are safe and comfortable seems to be a betrayal of its lifesaving mission. What many miss, however, is that the materialism and self-centeredness of the church is not a departure but the direct outcome of its narrowly defined mission and vision of the future. For nearly a century Christians have been told to separate from the world and await the end of all things. This message appealed to our desire for safety and lured many to seek refuge in the safe harbor of the church. When the end did not come, the urgency of the warning faded. The Rapture did not occur. The world was not destroyed. And the self-focused desire for safety that led many Christians to seek refuge at the beginning slowly became a self-focused desire for comfort. We cannot win converts with a self-centered message and then be appalled when they became self-centered Christians.

It should now be clear that the path of evacuation is fueled by fear. Like frightened turtles, Christians walking this road to Futureville pull inward to protect themselves from the dangers outside. They fear becoming tainted by a condemned world. They fear the suffering and discomfort of God's judgment. They fear the decline of the world into depravity and sin. Believing the world is beyond saving, they see evacuation as a pathway based on the narrow hope of escape. The Rapture will transport the redeemed off this planet to inhabit paradise while everyone else goes down with the ship.

Purpose, like hope, on this road is extremely limited. The only meaningful life is the one spent rescuing others from the impending doom. The fruit of every other work is destined for the flames. Until the end comes, however, those committed to evacuation make themselves comfortable by occupying a Christian replica of the world they someday hope to escape.

# FIVE
# RESURRECTION

## THE GAP

In order to appreciate the full beauty of Cape Town, South Africa, one must view it from the sea. Rising from the waters of the South Atlantic, the city's layers build upon one another—colonial stone structures along the coast, then glass and steel skyscrapers, then rolling foothills of green farmland and vineyards, and finally the breathtaking wall of amethyst stone known as Table Mountain, which serves as the canvas for the whole scene.

The stunning beauty of Cape Town makes the horrors the city has hosted, and all of South Africa, appear that much uglier. The policy of apartheid divided races, disempowered millions of people, and sparked countless cycles of violence and retribution. For his efforts to end apartheid and establish justice, Nelson Mandela became a prisoner of the state for twenty-seven years. I was familiar with Mandela's story before traveling to South Africa, but being there helped me sense the agony of his imprisonment in a new way. It wasn't the tiny, barren cell he occupied with only a bucket for a toilet, or the backbreaking physical labor he endured in the quarry that got my attention. It was the view. Nelson Mandela spent most of his imprisonment on Robben Island, seven kilometers off the coast of Cape Town. The island is blessed with an unparalleled view of the city.

Throughout his imprisonment, Mandela could see the remarkable beauty of his home, but he could not reach it. Seven kilometers of hostile waters barred the way. As a result, Robben Island provided a peculiar kind of torture shared by few other prisons.[1] It allowed Mandela to see freedom but not possess it. Still, Nelson Mandela was not without hope. To cope with the gap between his vision and his reality, he did something very ordinary. He planted a garden. After years of petitioning the authorities, they finally permitted their most famous inmate to cultivate a small garden in one corner of the prison yard. He started with a few seeds collected from around the island and spent hours every day working his plot, studying growing techniques, and testing fertilizers—pigeon manure worked particularly well. Over time his garden became a refuge for both prisoners and guards who shared in its bounty of vegetables and flowers.

Mandela later explained why the garden became so important to him. "To plant a seed, watch it grow, to tend it and then harvest it, offered a simple but enduring satisfaction. The sense of being the custodian of this small patch of earth offered a small taste of freedom."[2] He could not transform Robben Island into the freedom and beauty of Cape Town, but he could cultivate a small patch of ground to reflect the order, beauty, and abundance his soul longed for across the gap.

Mandela's garden reminds us that there exists an uncrossable sea between the world we desire and the one we occupy. Just as Mandela could see Cape Town but could not reach it, so we can see in our imaginations the world as it should be—the garden city of God—but it does not match the barren wilderness we experience in the present. Between today and tomorrow lie the cold waters of reality. The path of evolution promised to build a bridge across this gap through human ingenuity and progress, but history has proven evolution's bridge cannot span the divide. The path of evacuation promised to launch a few fortunate souls off the island, leaving the others behind; for most it offered no hope at all.

The way of Jesus, however, is different. Like Nelson Mandela's prison-yard garden, Jesus came to cultivate a living hope right among us. Rather than evolution or evacuation, through the incarnation God took on flesh and entered into the wilderness of the world, and there he started to cultivate order, beauty, and abundance that could be experienced in the present. He reached across the gap of time and space to grab hold of the garden city of tomorrow, and he yanked pieces of it into the wilderness of today. Jesus came to give us a glimpse of Futureville in our midst.

Consider the cultivating Jesus did. When chaos threatened his friends with a storm, he merely spoke a word and restored order to creation. When the ugliness of disease and death ravaged bodies, he restored beauty and wholeness. When the crowds did not have enough to eat, he created an abundance of food with a few loaves of bread and fish. People began to believe that through Jesus, God's perfect garden city was becoming reality. The gap was growing smaller, and Futureville was within their reach.

For some, however, the chaos, ugliness, and scarcity of the wilderness were too overwhelming. They could not see the small patches of hope Jesus was busy cultivating. John the Baptist had this problem while locked away in Herod's dungeon. Seeing only the evil and injustice of the world, John began to doubt. He sent his friends to Jesus with a question: "Are you the one?"[3] Rather than rebuking John for his weak faith, Jesus graciously offered him a glimpse of the garden through his friends. "Go and tell John what you have seen and heard: the blind receive their sight, the lame walk, lepers are cleansed, and the deaf hear, the dead are raised up, the poor have good news preached to them."[4]

This same pattern continues today. When we gather on Sunday with other Christians, some of us come having seen glimpses of Futureville in our world. We come with testimonies of how Jesus is still at work cultivating order, beauty, and abundance. But there are others who gather, like John, racked with doubt because they can see nothing but wilderness. Some gather having put their faith in the paths of evolution or evacuation, and rather than producing hope and purpose, they have found only despair and defeat. For this reason Scripture tells us not to neglect meeting together but to encourage one another.[5] We are to help one another see the reality of God's ongoing presence and power amid the wilderness of our world. We are to open one another's eyes to the order, beauty, and abundance Christ is cultivating today, and when we see these things, we are filled with courage. The glimpses come through the stories of our brothers and sisters, through the preaching of the Scriptures, through the grace and testimony of the Eucharist, through the beauty of songs and symbols, and through the sharing of gifts. When the church gathers for worship, we are reaching forward and yanking pieces of Futureville into the present just as Jesus did for John.

Still, the incarnation of Christ among us and his cultivation of order, beauty, and abundance is not all there is to this third pathway to Futureville. Jesus came to give us more than mere glimpses of hope. He came to unleash a power that would make all things new.

## THE PROTOTYPE

Why Sunday? In the Roman Empire, Sunday was akin to our Monday; it was the first day of the workweek. Why would the earliest Christians choose to gather for worship at such an inconvenient time? Saturday would have been a much better option, given its acceptance as a day of rest since the time of Moses. The Sunday school answer, if you will forgive the cliché, is that Jesus was resurrected on Sunday; therefore, Christians gathered to celebrate their risen King on that day every week.

This answer, however, begs another question. Why was Jesus raised on a Sunday? To answer that, we must have some familiarity with the Jewish account of creation from the first chapter of Genesis. There we read of God ordering the cosmos in six days and resting on the seventh. This text is where Jews find the basis for their practice of Sabbath—resting from work on the seventh day of the week. This text also identifies Sunday as the first day of God's creative work. Here we discover the importance of Jesus' Sunday resurrection. N. T. Wright explained:

> Easter [Sunday] functions as the beginning of the new creation. The Word through whom all things were made is now the Word through whom all things are remade. So far from being an odd or isolated supernatural event . . . Jesus' resurrection is to be seen as the beginning of the new world, the first day of the new week, the unveiling of the prototype of what God is now going to accomplish in the rest of the world.[6]

Many Christians acknowledge that Jesus' resurrection marked his victory over death and the ultimate validation of his divine identity. They also celebrate his resurrection as proof for their own hope for eternal life. Because of Jesus' resurrection we can say with the apostle Paul, "O death, where is your victory? O death, where is your sting?"[7] These understandings of the resurrection are certainly good and true, but we often fail to see beyond the individual implications of Easter Sunday. Seeking to correct this myopia, N. T. Wright points us to the cosmic scope of Jesus' resurrection as inaugurating the re-creation of all things—an act that parallels God's original creative work on the first Sunday in Genesis 1.

The bond between Easter Sunday and the re-creation of the cosmos is a truth rooted in the New Testament. In the same passage where Paul linked Jesus' resurrection with our individual hope for new life (1 Corinthians 15), he also acknowledged its cosmic implications. Paul repeatedly refered to the risen Christ as the "firstfruits."[8] He meant that Jesus' resurrection was the start and the pattern for what was to follow; he was the first fruit picked in a much larger harvest that is now underway. To use Wright's language, Jesus' resurrection was the prototype for God's new, creative work. Paul split this re-creation into three parts. Jesus has been raised first, he said, and "then at his coming those who belong to Christ" will be raised.[9] Finally, all God's enemies will be destroyed, including death itself, and "all things" will be made subject to God.[10]

Like the creation account in Genesis, which began but did not end on Sunday, God's re-creation began on Easter Sunday with Jesus' resurrection but continues to unfold. According to Paul's logic in 1 Corinthians 15, re-creation began with Christ, flows to his church, and finds completion in the cosmos. The power of Christ's resurrection that was unleashed on Easter will eventually bring new life to all that God has made.

We discover this same pattern in Romans 8. Speaking to Christians enduring hardship, Paul framed their suffering in light of what was to come:

> For I consider that the sufferings of this present time are not worth comparing with the glory that is to be revealed to us. For the creation waits with eager longing for the revealing of the sons of God. For the creation was subjected to futility, not willingly, but because of him who subjected it, in hope that the creation itself will be set free from its bondage to corruption and obtain the freedom of the glory of the children of God. For we know that the whole creation has been groaning together in the pains of childbirth until now. And not only the creation, but we ourselves, who have the firstfruits of the Spirit, groan inwardly as we wait eagerly for adoption as sons, the redemption of our bodies.[11]

Here we find a remarkable link between our coming resurrection, the "redemption of our bodies," and the resurrection of creation itself. Paul acknowledged that while we have been reborn spiritually through faith in Christ, our physical rebirth is yet to come and will occur when Christ returns. But we are not the only ones longing for that day. Paul said the creation itself waits with eager longing because it, too, will be set free to share in the same freedom and glory we will experience.

The resurrection power of Christ will transform us and the broken world we occupy into Futureville. Like Jesus and his people, the earth itself will be set free from sin, reconciled to God, and glorified. To return to Nelson Mandela's prison metaphor, imagine the seven kilometers separating Robben Island from Cape Town being removed, the two united into one land, and Mandela's tiny prison-yard garden transformed into the full order, beauty, and goodness of Cape Town. In this vision Robben Island will not be abandoned or destroyed but redeemed. This is the great hope inaugurated on Easter Sunday that will find fulfillment on a coming day when all things are put under God's rule and he is "all in all."[12] The world itself will be made new, the gap removed, and heaven and earth united—the very image the apostle John saw when the holy city descended from heaven to earth in Revelation 21. Futureville is neither an ethereal heaven nor a replaced earth. It is the union of heaven and earth into a restored and glorified cosmos occupied by God and his people.

This remarkable idea is altogether different from the path offered by either evolution or evacuation. The hope of evolution was found to be extremely unsatisfying, as any positive progress by humanity has been tainted by equal advancements in our capacity for evil. The hope of evacuation was found to be extremely limited—reserved only for the souls of those rescued off our sinking world while the rest of creation was abandoned to destruction. What we find in the New Testament, however, is neither an unsatisfying nor limiting hope. We discover the hope of resurrection extending to all things—the entire cosmos that God created in the beginning and declared "good." We find the message that Christ came not merely to save sinners from a doomed planet, but to rescue all that he created. As Paul wonderfully declared:

> He is the beginning, the firstborn from the dead, that in everything he might be preeminent. For in him all the fullness of God was pleased to dwell, and through him to reconcile to himself all things, whether on earth or in heaven, making peace by the blood of his cross.[13]

## THE "NEW"

If you are familiar with the Bible, or the popular literature produced by evacuation proponents, you may be wondering how the view of God reconciling all creation through the power of Jesus' resurrection jives with the idea of a "new heaven and new earth." The apostle John used this language when speaking of his vision of the garden city:

> Then I saw a *new heaven and a new earth*, for the first heaven and the first earth had passed away, and the sea was no more.[14]

The apostle Peter also used this wording:

> . . . the heavens will be set on fire and dissolved, and the heavenly bodies will melt as they burn! But according to his promise we are waiting for *new heavens and a new earth* in which righteousness dwells.[15]

These passages, among others, have fueled much of the evacuation viewpoint that God will destroy and replace the present creation. If this is the case, then it makes perfect sense to disengage from our world and await the new one that is to come. This interpretation raises two questions. First, if the risen Christ is the prototype of God's re-creation, why does Scripture speak of a new heaven and earth? And, second, if the apostles do not mean to communicate the replacement of our world with a new one, how should we then read these texts?

Let's begin with the resurrection. By referring to Jesus' resurrection as the "firstfruits" in 1 Corinthians 15, the apostle Paul was communicating that it was both the start and the pattern for what was to come. He made this explicit in verses 35 to 45, where he spoke of the nature of Jesus' resurrected body as a prototype for what our resurrected bodies will be like. He repeated this again in Romans, as did John in his first letter:

> For if we have been united with him in a death like his, we shall certainly be united with him in a resurrection like his.[16]
>
> Beloved, we are God's children now, and what we will be has not yet appeared; but we know that when he appears we shall be like him.[17]

And we have already seen from Romans 8 that the same resurrection glory that awaits us will be shared by the liberated cosmos:

> . . . the creation itself will be set free from its bondage to corruption and obtain the freedom of the glory of the children of God.[18]

If Jesus' resurrection is the prototype, then in order to understand the nature of our future resurrected bodies, as well as the future resurrected creation, we must look at the resurrected body of Jesus.

The first thing we recognize, both from the Gospel accounts of the resurrection and Paul's description of it in 1 Corinthians 15, is that Jesus' resurrected body was different. As Paul said, "What is sown is perishable; what is raised is imperishable. It is sown in dishonor; it is raised in glory. It is sown in weakness; it is raised in power. It is sown a natural body; it is raised a spiritual body."[19] Indeed, after the resurrection, Jesus exhibited characteristics he did not possess prior to death. He appeared and disappeared, moved through walls,[20] and ascended into the air.[21] His body defied the established laws of physics. From this we may conclude, as Paul did, that our future bodies, as well as the future of the cosmos, will be different from the present bodies and world we know. There will be discontinuity between the present age and the age to come. As Paul declared, when the day of Christ arrives, "we shall all be changed."[22]

Discontinuity is the quality most emphasized by the path of evacuation. It says there will be complete discontinuity between the present world and the world to come, with only the souls of the saved enduring from one to the other. This replacement theology, however, does not work when applied to the resurrection of Jesus. While his body was certainly changed, it was not replaced. Jesus was not given a new body and his old one discarded, as the evacuation path argues will happen to the earth. Jesus was not reincarnated; he was resurrected. Jesus' body was not replaced; it was raised. Scripture is unwavering on this point. The tomb was empty. If Jesus' body had been left to rot in the tomb and replaced, death would have still claimed a partial victory. By raising, not replacing, his body, Jesus showed his complete victory over every enemy. Death is given no consolation prize—not even the tortured body of a Nazarene carpenter. To prove this fact, the resurrected Jesus showed his disciples the wounds from his crucifixion. Thomas even touched the scars on his hands and side.[23] While his body was changed, it was still his body.

We may conclude from the New Testament that Jesus' resurrection exhibits both continuity and discontinuity. Resurrection results in a remarkable sameness and a radical transformation. When we apply this pattern to the world, as Paul did in both 1 Corinthians 15 and Romans 8, we see God's intent is to redeem this world (continuity) but also transform it to exhibit the characteristic of the perfected garden city (discontinuity). The earth you and I inhabit right now will someday become Futureville.

If the present world is to be redeemed and changed, how do we make sense of John and Peter speaking of a "new" heaven and earth? Translation is part of the challenge. The Greek word translated "new" in these texts is not *neos*, which means new in substance or time, but a more nuanced and complicated word—*kainos*, which can also carry the meaning of new in quality. If today I purchased a Darth Vader action figure at a toy store, I could say it is "new." The Greek word *neos* would apply here, meaning "young." If, however, I purchased a vintage Darth Vader action figure from 1977 still in its original packaging and unopened, I could not call this toy "young." Instead, I would say it is "new in condition." The word *kainos* would apply here. While this is an oversimplification of a more complicated issue of translation, the fact is when the New Testament speaks of a "new heaven and earth," we cannot automatically assume it means "young." By employing the word *kainos,* the writers can mean "new in quality," which is consistent with Paul's teaching and the pattern we see in Jesus' resurrection. His raised body was certainly new in quality, but it was not a newly created body that replaced his previous one. It was his body transformed to exhibit new qualities.

Paul used similar language when speaking of our newness in Christ. "If anyone is in Christ," he said, "he is a new creation. The old has passed away; behold, the new has come."[24] Here Paul was clearly speaking qualitatively, not substantively. I did not cease to be me when I put my trust in Christ, but I was changed and passed from death to life. To use language familiar to many, I was "born again." In John 3, where Jesus uses this phrase, he makes clear that he is speaking of a spiritual rebirth, not a physical one. Similarly, the new heaven and earth, like Jesus' new body and our newness in Christ, is not a material replacement of the current heaven and earth.

Instead, it is the radical transformation and re-creation of heaven and earth to reflect new qualities.

Consider the element carbon. Carbon is known as a polymorphic element because it exists naturally as two different substances: graphite and diamond. Both are chemically identical, but they do not appear or behave alike due to their structural differences. In graphite the carbon atoms form sheets of bonds, resulting in a substance that is opaque, brittle, and weak. Diamonds, however, are carbon atoms in a tetrahedral structure, creating a crystal that is translucent and harder than any substance on earth. You can buy a graphite pencil for a few pennies. A diamond containing the same amount of carbon, however, would be priceless.

Scripture seems to teach that the cosmos is polymorphic. In its current configuration the world is marked by chaos, ugliness, and scarcity. It groans under its bondage to death and decay.[25] But the day is approaching when the resurrection power of Christ will be unleashed and the cosmos itself will be changed. Rather than reading the fire imagery in 2 Peter 3:12–13 as utterly destroying the earth, instead we should understand fire to be a symbol of purification. Peter employed the metaphor of fire as a purifying force in the faith of Christ's people (1 Peter 1:7), and the purifying purpose of fire was described by Paul in 1 Corinthians 3:13 when speaking of the Day of Judgment. When Christ returns, therefore, we should not expect the earth to be destroyed but liberated from the curse as chaos, ugliness, and scarcity are purged away,[26] and the world is transformed into order, beauty, and abundance. The dark, broken creation will be made new and come to reflect the glory of its Creator and Redeemer. It will be the same world but raised to a new life. This is the resurrection path to Futureville.

## THE GARDENERS

The resurrection shows us that there is both truth and error in the paths of evolution and evacuation. Evolution placed the emphasis upon human progress—our ability to transform our world into Futureville. It left little space for the intervention of God, which is why some on the path of evolution decided God was an unnecessary relic from an earlier, superstitious age. Evacuation, on the other hand, relied entirely upon God's intervention to destroy and replace this world. It left no space for the contribution of humanity in his work of re-creation apart from issuing warnings that the end was near.

The way of resurrection, however, incorporates the most admirable elements from each of these incomplete paths. First, resurrection requires God's direct and miraculous intervention. We clearly do not possess the power to raise the dead; this can only come from the Author of life. We need God's power to come and set us and our world free from the curse of evil and death. In other words, we must rely upon God's grace. Second, the fact that resurrection includes continuity means that what we do today may endure into the age to come. Just as Jesus' identity, appearance, and even scars remained after his resurrection, might our cultivation of this earth also be preserved?

Might our work, that which we do in communion with God and through his power, be taken up and incorporated into his liberated creation even as the effects of evil are purged away? Can our efforts to manifest God's kingdom now, as the path of evolution says, endure for eternity?

Apart from linking Jesus' resurrection and the future transformation of the earth, Scripture offers additional evidence that our present work really does matter. Paul spoke of the quality of each man's work being tested on the Day of Judgment.[27] Some work, being of poor quality or inconsistent with the character of God, will be burned up. Works of high quality, which he compared to gold, silver, and precious stones, will endure the testing and survive.

Similarly, John's vision of the New Jerusalem includes a scene where the rulers of the earth bring the glory of the nations into the city. What are these glories? Drawing from both Isaiah's vision of the Holy City and John's Revelation, Richard Mouw explores this question in his book *When the Kings Come Marching In*. He argues that rather than destroying the artifacts and creations of pagan cultures, God will instead purify and redeem them for use in Futureville for his glory. Mouw wrote:

> When the kings come marching in, then, they bring the best of their nations—even the cultural goods that had been deployed against God and his people. The final vision of the City is one filled, not just with God's glory and presence, not just with his own stunningly beautiful

> architectural designs, not just with redeemed persons from every cultural background—but with redeemed human culture too.[28]

The things we create and the work we pursue in this world will have a place and even a use in Futureville—and rather than sitting on clouds singing hymns for eternity, Mouw said, the activities of culture will continue.

> The contents of the City will be more akin to our present cultural patterns than is usually acknowledged in discussions of the afterlife. Isaiah pictures the Holy City as a center of commerce, a place that receives the vessels, goods, and currency of commercial activity. . . . Isaiah is, in contemporary jargon, interested in the future of "corporate structures" and "cultural patterns."[29]

This is an incredible notion. In Futureville, King David may someday admire Michelangelo's statue of himself, Handel may well perform his *Messiah* for the Messiah, and the work we are gifted and called to engage in the present age may continue into the next, albeit in a redeemed and untainted form. Knowing exactly what will endure and what will not is an impossible question to answer and would take us into speculation beyond the revelation of Scripture. From our exploration of the Bible and the path of resurrection, however, I believe we can define three principles:

1. Discontinuity means anything inconsistent with God's character and his plan for creation will be purged away in the age to come.
2. Continuity means the things of this world that are consistent with God's character and plan will endure.
3. Our efforts to manifest Futureville in the present by cultivating order, beauty, and abundance matter both now and for eternity.

We have a role to play in God's plan to unite heaven and earth, to advance the story of the world to culmination, and to see the earth cultivated into the garden city. In other words, God's original intent for humanity has been restored in us through Jesus Christ. In the beginning, God called humanity to fill the earth and subdue it. He commissioned his image-bearers to carry his order, beauty, and abundance to the ends of the earth. This mission, frustrated and derailed by our rebellion, can now be reengaged as we are reconciled to God through the cross and made new in Christ.

Jesus came as the Master Gardener cultivating his kingdom in the prison yard of this world. He offered glimpses of Futureville through his manifestations of order, beauty, and abundance, but this cultivation did not end when he ascended to the Father. Through the presence of his Spirit, we have become gardeners as well. Jesus may have fed multitudes by a miracle, but Christians in the book of Acts created an abundance of food by sharing their resources. Jesus overcame chaos with order by calming the sea, but his people overcame chaos by manifesting a new order that valued the dignity of all—rich and poor, male and female, Jew and Greek—and invited all into a right relationship with God. Jesus revealed beauty as he healed bodies and reflected the glory of God, but his followers contributed to the beauty of the world and reflected the beauty of God by worshipping him with songs, hymns, and spiritual songs.

Like Jesus, we are gardeners cultivating the world to look increasingly like the garden city of God. We are called to build Futureville today. We work our patches of the prison yard, not simply as a symbol of hope as we await our eventual escape. We do it in anticipation of the day when the gap between Robben Island and Cape Town will be erased—the day when heaven and earth will be united, and the order, beauty, and abundance we have cultivated will become part of the world of tomorrow. This is the great hope that animates our lives in Christ.

But until then, how do we know what part of this world to cultivate? What patches of the prison yard are ours to till? Where do we focus our energy and time, and what exactly do we seek to grow there? These are the questions of purpose that were so easily answered by the paths of evolution and evacuation based on their understanding of what will endure. Evolution said our purpose was to change society, and evacuation said our purpose was to save souls; but if "all things" matter to God,[30] how do we know what work truly matters? To answer that question we must turn our attention to a wonderful teaching once cherished by the church but largely ignored in our day—vocation.

# SIX

# VOCATION

## THE CALLS

God did not create the cosmos and then retire into full-time church work. If God had a business card, I think it would say, "The Universe Business." He is engaged in the movement of the most infinitesimal particles as well as the grandest achievements of human history. He cares about it all, and as we discovered in the last chapter, through Jesus Christ he is reconciling all of it to himself. The question, therefore, is not, what part of the world does God ultimately care about?—which is what the paths of evolution and evacuation focused on—but rather, what part of his world am I supposed to engage? This is the question that we encounter on the path of resurrection.

The answer is found in the theological idea of vocation.

Most people do not consider vocation a theological concept. That's because the word is now used as a synonym for one's profession or career, but that is not what it originally meant. It comes from the Latin word *vocaré*, meaning "to call." Centuries ago the word only applied to bishops, priests, and monks—those occupying offices within the hierarchy of the Roman Catholic Church. It was believed that the clergy had been called by God; they alone had a vocation while everyone else merely worked.

The idea dates back to Eusebius, the bishop of Caesarea in the fourth century. He wrote that Christ had established two ways of life: the "perfect life" and the "permitted life."[1] The perfect life was the one God called the clergy to—a life of prayer, worship, and service to Christ through the church. Other occupations, while not prohibited, carried less dignity. The labor of farmers, artists, merchants, and homemakers was not evil, but neither was it blessed, and these roles were certainly not callings from God. After all, they were concerned with the things of earth, while the clergy were occupied with the things of heaven.[2]

Apart from isolated challenges, this hierarchy of labor endured within Western Christianity for a thousand years until the Protestant Reformation. Leaders like Martin Luther and John Calvin called Christians back to the authority of Scripture, and there they found no justification for the exaltation of the clergy or the demotion of other labor. Rather, they affirmed the priesthood of all believers—the notion that every Christian has direct communion with God through

Christ without the mediation of an earthly priest—and they expanded the Roman Catholic idea of vocation to include all people. They read in the New Testament that everyone should do "honest work with his own hands, so that he may have something to share with anyone in need."[3] This was more than a rebuke of laziness; it was an affirmation of work, including physical labor, as a way of blessing others and manifesting Christian love.

The Protestant Reformers also recognized that worship of God was not limited to one's time in a cathedral. God received glory in the ordinary activities of life—including work. As Paul instructed the Corinthians, "Whatever you do, do all to the glory of God."[4] From these writings and others in Scripture they concluded that all work was to be seen as noble, Christ-honoring, and valuable. Luther wrote:

> The works of monks and priests, however holy and arduous they be, do not differ one whit in the sight of God from the works of the rustic laborer in the field or the woman going about her household tasks, but that all works are measured before God by faith alone. . . . Indeed, the menial housework of a manservant or maidservant is often more acceptable to God than all the fastings and other works of a monk or priest, because the monk or priest lacks faith.[5]

With this recalibration of the doctrine of vocation, many came to view their labors differently, not as a menial labor to be endured, but as a God-ordained calling to be pursued with religious zeal. It resulted in a new devotion to work that historians referred to as the Protestant work ethic, and it was coupled with a vision that Christ was actively engaged in every part of the world—not just the church. As the Dutch theologian and prime minister Abraham Kuyper wrote, "In the total expanse of human life there is not a single square inch of which the Christ, who alone is sovereign, does not declare, 'That is mine!'"[6] This new understanding of work meant things suddenly mattered that the church had long ago abandoned. Commerce, agriculture, government, and the home became legitimate, even holy arenas in which to serve God, and a person determined where to serve the same way clergy did—by listening for Christ's call upon his life.

Despite the helpful correction to Eusebius's two-class view of vocation, the Protestant view still had a weakness. Some Christians might come to view their God-given work as all-important. In other words, the Protestant view of vocation could make work into an idol. The Puritans recognized this danger. To guard against it, they articulated a more nuanced theology of vocation by recognizing each person had multiple callings that needed to be held together. They understood that every Christian had a highest calling, a common calling, and a specific calling.

The Puritans preached that each person's highest calling was not his labor, but rather Christ himself. As Os Guinness wonderfully articulated, "First and foremost we are called to Someone (God), not to something (such as motherhood, politics, or teaching) or to somewhere (such as the inner city or

Outer Mongolia)."[7] This is an idea I addressed extensively in my previous book *With: Reimagining the Way You Relate to God*. There I wrote of the temptation to build our lives around what we do for God rather than our communion with him, and how the subtle but toxic idolatry of ministry is pervasive within the contemporary church. The only way to overcome it is to find our greatest joy in Christ, and in his presence discover the divine mystery that his joy is made complete in us. In other words, God does not need us. He wants us.

Following our highest calling to live with Christ, the Puritans understood that all Christians also share a set of common callings. These are the many commands of Scripture that apply to all God's children in every time and place—instructions such as love one another, pray for those who persecute you, forgive those who wrong you, give to those in need, honor your father and mother, do not steal, do not covet, do not commit adultery, be prepared to share about your hope in Christ, and hundreds of other commands. Our common callings are what our Christian communities focus upon almost exclusively today. The reason for this is simple—common callings are easy to discover. One simply opens the Bible and reads them. Having read Ephesians, Pastor Brian can stand before his congregation on Sunday with divine authority and say, "Husbands, love your wives." This is a common calling for all married Christians, but Pastor Brian cannot cite chapter and verse to proclaim a specific calling like, "Sally, go to law school." A specific calling, which is what we often mean when we use the word *vocation*, requires Sally to live in communion with God and discern his call directly. While her specific calling may be blessed and confirmed by members of her community, as Paul and Barnabas experienced in Acts 13, it cannot be discovered without the illuminating role of God's Spirit in her life.

Herein lies the problem. In many of our Christian communities there is a functional denial of the Holy Spirit. We may affirm the Spirit as a doctrinal truth, but the reality of his presence is often ignored. As a result, Christians are not equipped to engage their highest calling (communion with God) or to discern their specific calling (vocation). What remains is the one thing the church can access without the Spirit's presence—the Scripture. While God-given and certainly good, our common callings as captured in the Bible only constitute one facet of our Christian lives, and without the presence of the Spirit we will remain powerless to follow these commands. For this reason, if Christians do not grasp their highest calling to live in vibrant, continual communion with God through the indwelling presence of the Holy Spirit, then neither our common nor specific callings can be properly engaged. If we get our highest callings right, however, and welcome the reality of the Spirit into our lives, then in most cases our other callings take care of themselves.[8]

## THE DIVIDE

By ignoring the doctrines of our highest and specific callings, the contemporary church has also found itself employing a leadership model that looks more like a corporation in which a single visionary leader determines everyone's work. Drawn by the efficiency and success of corporations, many pastors think of themselves as CEOs of an organization. They articulate a mission, set goals, rally people and resources around themselves, and finally align them all to accomplish a single task. This model would look familiar to Eusebius and would probably be affirmed by him. In it the church leader is the individual hearing from God, and the work of the institutional church is what ultimately matters. Whether a person is a nurse, farmer, architect, or shopkeeper is irrelevant, as long as she is onboard with the church's vision in her free time and contributes to it. A person's value, in this model, is determined by how closely she aligns with the institutional church's vision and mission.

Often the mission articulated in this model is rooted in Scripture and part of our common callings, such as the call to "make disciples" or to be "witnesses of Jesus Christ." Who would disagree with the importance of these works? Still, when these callings are untethered from our highest call (communion with God) or the specific vocations Christ has given to each of his followers, it can do great damage. When this happens, the institutional church's work soon becomes all-consuming, and many Christians develop a suspicion that the church's leaders really only care about advancing their institution's agenda. They begin to feel like the leaders are using them rather than loving them.

I have been guilty of this. For years I served as a teaching pastor at my church, but then left the pastoral team to pursue a calling outside the institutional church. For the first time since graduating from seminary I found myself in the pews more often than in the pulpit, and it changed my perspective. Working as an editor for a Christian magazine, traveling more often, and juggling a young family left little flexible time in my schedule. There was simply no way I could participate in everything the church was asking me to while also fulfilling the specific calling I believed God had given me to pursue outside the church.

Within a few months I understood how most of the people in my congregation felt, and I came to see how insensitive and guilt-inducing many of my past sermons must have been. For years I had called them to give more time, money, and energy to the work of the institutional church in sermon after sermon with little or no understanding or affirmation of their specific callings in the world. I had inadvertently created a secular versus sacred divide in which the "sacred" calling of the church was pitted against their "secular" callings in the world. I never said this explicitly in a sermon, but I often implied it.

Months later, when I was invited to preach again, my message included an apology for my failure to understand the value of work outside the church. The sermon was met with shouts of "Amen!"—not a common occurrence in our predominantly Anglo suburban congregation, but understandable because I had finally broken through my narrow focus upon our common callings to see that Christ had also issued specific callings to each of his children. I had finally seen the folly of the sacred/secular divide that had dominated my approach to ministry for years.

Resistance to the sacred/secular divide, and the expectation that one's first commitment should be to the institutional church, is especially evident among the young adults I have engaged. While earlier generations of Christians may have valued the idea of surrendering their lives and fortunes to an institution, the young today do not. In fact, they are increasingly suspicious of all large organizations. As Laura Hansen, an assistant professor of sociology at Western New England University, said, "We lost [faith] in the media: Remember Walter Cronkite? We lost it in our culture: You can't point to a movie star who might inspire us, because we know too much about them. We lost it in politics, because we know too much about politicians' lives. We've lost it—that basic sense of trust and confidence—in everything."[9] The church is no different. According to Gallop, forty years ago 68 percent of Americans reported having a strong or high confidence in the church. Today it is only 44 percent, and among the young it is even lower.[10]

This generation's lack of response to the institutional church's call has left many pastors flummoxed. They mistakenly believe it is a matter of style. "If we just change our music, add some candles, and turn up the 'cool' factor, more young people will engage," they say. Others blame it on immaturity. In chapter 1, I mentioned the pastor who asked me, "How do I get a generation that doesn't believe in commitment to commit to the church?" I don't believe the problem is style or immaturity; it is a church that has lost a theology of vocation. We fail to see beyond our common callings to the believer's highest call (God) or specific call (vocation).

Young people, perhaps more than previous generations,

have a strong sense of their specific callings. They believe God has called them into business, the arts, government, the household, education, the media, the social sector, or health care, and they are often very committed to these venues of cultural engagement. But when their specific callings are not acknowledged by the institutional church, and instead only our common callings or the goals of the organization are extolled, the young are unlikely to engage. Rather than embracing the fullness of the Christian life comprising multiple facets—highest, common, and specific callings—the church unknowingly communicates that following Christ is a tension between sacred callings and secular work. You must sacrifice your specific, secular calling to do more of the sacred work the institutional church says really matters. This guilt-laden message is one a young, jaded generation is much less likely to tolerate. It is interpreted as a self-serving power play by church leaders even if, like me, they never intended it to be. The error of Eusebius is alive and well in the Western church today.

Does this mean the institutional church should stop emphasizing our common callings or its evangelistic mission? Absolutely not! Rather, it is vital that the church rediscover the God-given dignity of all callings and how they fit together. It is not the pastor's task to wrestle more people away from "secular" engagements in order to help him accomplish "sacred" work, but to erase these categories in the lives of those he leads in order that Christ might come to reign over all parts of their lives.

Echoing the Protestant reformers and the Puritans, Dallas

Willard recognizes the danger of dividing our work into departments and the destructive illusion it fosters. He said:

> There truly is no division between sacred and secular except what we have created. And that is why the division of the legitimate roles and functions of human life into the sacred and secular does incalculable damage to our individual lives and the cause of Christ. Holy people must stop going into "church work" as their natural course of action and take up holy orders in farming, industry, law, education, banking, and journalism with the same zeal previously given to evangelism or to pastoral and missionary work.[11]

If we are to embrace this united view, then we must find a different model of church leadership, as well as a new way to affirm the value of each person's specific call within our Christian communities.

## THE QUARTERMASTER

"Right, now pay attention." Few people spoke to James Bond with more condescension than his quartermaster—better known simply as Q. Bond's interactions with Q were often my favorite scenes in the 007 movies, and they followed a predictable formula. Having been given his orders by M, the head of the British secret service, Bond then reported to Q to receive the gizmos, gadgets, and guns necessary to accomplish his mission. Bond's casual disrespect for the quartermaster's work created a playful tension between the two and provoked Q's frustrated calls to, "Pay attention, Double-O-Seven!"

The pattern evident within Her Majesty's Secret Service fits nicely with what Scripture says about the role of leaders in the church. While the popular model of ministry today views pastors more like M—the organizational chief who determines the agents' missions—the New Testament presents a model of church leadership that looks more like Q. The apostle Paul said:

> And [Christ] gave the apostles, the prophets, the evangelists, the shepherds and teachers, to equip the saints for the work of ministry, for building up the body of Christ, until we all attain to the unity of the faith and of the knowledge of the Son of God.[12]

Like Bond's quartermaster, leaders are to "equip" Christ's people. This equipping is first applied to our common calling to "[build] up the body of Christ." In other words, leaders equip us to serve one another within the community of Christians so that we may all grow in our communion with Christ. Here's another way of thinking about church leaders: the pastor's specific calling (to equip the saints) allows us to accomplish our common calling (to build up the church family), so that we all attain our highest calling (to live in unity with Christ).

In this model of leadership, however, the church leader is not given the mandate to determine each believer's specific calling. The pastor is not like M—the one determining the mission for each of God's "special agents." While we all have common callings that can be known and articulated by a pastor, as previously discussed, determining each person's specific calling is a task reserved for God alone. For example, before ascending to the Father, Jesus called Peter to shepherd his disciples. Three times Jesus told Peter to "feed" or "tend" his sheep. In addition, the Lord said that Peter's specific calling would include martyrdom. Perhaps Peter was less than thrilled with this career path, because immediately after hearing it he noticed another disciple, John, and asked Jesus about his specific calling. The Lord swiftly rebuked Peter, "If it is my will that he remain until I come, what is that to you? You follow me!"[13] In this scene we see Peter's temptation to overstep his equipping role of feeding the sheep. He wanted to know, and perhaps influence, John's specific calling; but Jesus made it clear that this kind of calling was not Peter's responsibility. Similarly when Jesus said, "The harvest is plentiful, but the laborers are few,"[14] he did not tell his apostles to call or send more workers. Instead, he instructed them to "pray earnestly to the Lord of the harvest to send out laborers."[15] Calling is the Lord's prerogative. He is the head of the church, directing each of his servants to the work he has determined.

This requires a different model of leadership within the church. Rather than a command-and-control CEO model, where the pastor seeks to align every person and resource around the church's institutional goals, leaders should be equipping God's people to fulfill the specific callings they have received from the Lord because these specific callings are a significant way

God's work is manifested in the world. As Paul said earlier in his letter to the Ephesians, "We are his workmanship, created in Christ Jesus for good works, which God prepared beforehand, that we should walk in them."[16] Some of these "good works" fall into the category of our common calling, but many more of them are going to be the specific works assigned to each of God's children. This model of leadership would also nullify the objections and cynicism of a generation that views the church as self-serving. Rather than simply recruiting Christians to serve within the confines of the institutional church, the equipping model of leadership helps each person discover and fulfill Christ's calling for his or her life in his world.

Imagine a Christian community where followers of Christ are not merely focused upon church-based programs, but they are taught how to commune with Christ and glorify him in business, the arts, medicine, education, and every other channel of the culture where he has called them. Such a church would exist not to advance its own agenda but to advance the common good. Each person would know what part of God's world he or she is called to cultivate with the order, beauty, and abundance of Futureville. Their callings would all be diverse, occurring in different parts of the world and in various channels of culture, but every calling would be held in esteem by the church as coming from Christ and as part of his plan to redeem all things.

As Christians are equipped for these callings, their good works would benefit not only the church but everything and everyone in the community. Imagine Christian educators bringing order, beauty, and abundance to schools so students and their families thrive. Imagine Christian business leaders cultivating industries that value people, pay them fairly, and steward natural resources. Imagine Christian artists creating works of beauty that lift the spirits of those who have endured war or disease. Imagine Christian civic leaders passing just laws to ensure evil is restrained and life-giving order is possible. Such Christians would not only bring growth to our world, but they would also be cultivating the presence of Futureville today. They would serve as signs of God's presence in the world and his mission to redeem all things through the power of the resurrection of Christ. As Dorothy Sayers said, "Christian people, and particularly perhaps the Christian clergy, must get it firmly into their heads that when a man or woman is called to a particular job of secular work, that is as true a vocation as though he or she were called to specifically religious work."[17]

The paths of evolution and evacuation have no use for a theology of vocation, which explains why the idea of vocation has virtually disappeared within the contemporary church. These paths, and the leaders who promote them, have predetermined what work is important. One values social transformation, and the other values saving souls. If God is going about the redemption of all things, however, and this redemption was inaugurated with Jesus' resurrection, then hearing his call for our lives takes on unparalleled importance. His call is how we discover what part of the world we are called to cultivate to reflect the values of Futureville. But receiving our specific calls can only happen through the presence of the Holy Spirit and when leadership in the church is focused upon equipping God's people rather than using them.

Having reintroduced an understanding of vocation, we will now look at what can happen when God's people view their work in the world as a divine calling. We will see how the order, beauty, and abundance of Futureville is being cultivated in our world today.

# SEVEN

# ORDER

## THE IMAGE

"I view myself more as a father than a police officer," said Sergeant Mike Geiger of the Portland, Oregon, police department. Geiger leads Portland's trafficking unit and successfully campaigned in 2009 to shift the city's response to better protect children from sexual predators. Rather than viewing child prostitutes as complicit, the police now view them as victims. Thanks to Geiger, soliciting sex from a minor is now categorized as a major crime and investigated by detectives. "Our children are not complicit. It's not just a policy shift," he says. "It's a whole shift in thinking."

An investigative report in 2010 labeled Portland "the national hub for child sex trafficking." Sergeant Geiger is trying to change that. Leading his team of detectives in cooperation with the FBI, he tracks down victims, moves them to shelters for recovery, and prosecutes their pimps. Geiger recognizes that his calling to protect the innocent and to seek justice is rooted to his faith in Christ. "When we talk about these vulnerable people, my faith dictates that we protect and nurture them. Jesus' warning about the millstone highlights the inherent value of all children."[1]

Sergeant Geiger represents one of the ways Futureville is being cultivated in our world today. The future garden city of God will be a place where no evil or injustice abides; it will see the world perfectly ordered so all things may flourish. Those who belong to Christ and have experienced the renewing power of his resurrection, however, are not content to wait passively for this future to arrive. They are cultivating the order of Futureville now in anticipation of what is to come. Sergeant Geiger is called to pursue order as a police officer in Portland. He is faithfully cultivating his part of the earth by pursuing justice, restoring victims, and ensuring that the city of Portland protects the innocent and vulnerable.

The instinct for order is not limited to those called to criminal justice. It is part of the image of God imprinted upon every person. Children appear to be agents of chaos. They enter our lives like tiny weapons of mass destruction that destroy our well-ordered existences, but researchers insist their young brains thrive where there is order, routine, and predictability. As any new mother knows, getting a baby on a schedule of sleeping and eating is not only critical for the health of the child but also for the sanity of the parents. What adults interpret as destructive behavior by most children, say researchers, is really exploratory learning. The process of picking up objects, tasting them, and even throwing them across the room is how a toddler's brain discovers patterns and begins to makes sense of the world. In other words, a young child begins to order her world by destroying ours.

Artist M. C. Escher, best known for drawing optical illusions, said, "We adore chaos because we love to produce order."[2] We were created to order. This happens when a scientist discerns a new principle from what appeared to be a random universe. It happens when a community leader organizes citizens to accomplish a task. It happens when a child uses blocks to construct a tower. Whenever we create systems of management or categories of organization, or we build more complex structures from simple ones, we are ordering, and in such actions we reflect the image of our Creator.

The opening narrative of Genesis reveals God producing order from a primordial sea of chaos. He separated sea from sky, earth from water, darkness from light. He established boundaries, categories, and limits for the various elements of the cosmos, and then he filled these demarcated realms. The heavens he populated with celestial bodies. The seas he filled with fish and the skies with birds. After creating the man and woman he invited them to join him in his ongoing ordering of the planet. They were to "fill the earth and subdue it."[3] Humanity was to replicate the order of Eden to the ends of the earth, and the man began by naming the animals—an act of ordering.

The pursuit of order is a God-ordained instinct imprinted upon our species. Just as birds fly and fish swim, humans order. Stone and sand we order into bricks. Bricks we order into buildings. Buildings we order into cities. Cities we order into civilizations. Yet the biblical idea of ordering is more than assembling raw materials into fabricated goods. As we explored in chapter 2, God ordered the garden of Eden to be a realm of shalom—a place of comprehensive flourishing where all things thrive to their fullest potential. All things had to be in proper relationship to one another for this to happen. Humans with God, humans with one another, and humans with creation. There is a relational as well as a material dimension to ordering.

The ancient Hebrews had a word to describe the right ordering of relationships—*sedeq*. We translate the word as "righteousness" or "justice," but the word denotes more than the abstract notion of virtue. It is the "right standing and consequent right behavior within a community."[4] Righteousness is about the proper ordering of relationships so that flourishing is possible. *Sedeq* is exactly what we see in the beginning of creation. The newly ordered world is declared by God to be "very good." All things are rightly ordered for flourishing, beginning with humanity's relationship with God. Under his authority and in communion with him, humanity was positioned to continue the ordering of the world as it grew to produce ever more flourishing.

As outlined in chapter 2, however, humans severed their relationship with God and triggered a disastrous chain reaction that shattered the shalom of creation and disrupted the proper ordering of the cosmos. In Genesis 3, we discover how humanity's unrighteousness—the transgression of the human-divine relationship—resulted in the breakdown of every other relationship. The bond between the man and woman would be marked by strife rather than fruitful collaboration, and rather than submitting to the ordering of humanity, the earth would now resist their efforts. What God intended to be our creative work became frustrating toil. So much of our labor in this world is now a battle against the forces of chaos. What we build soon falls. What we order quickly decays.

The disordering impact of sin, however, is not only evident in our world. It has also warped the image of God we each carry. When we use our power to establish right relationships and arrange for the flourishing of all things, we project the image of God faithfully to his world. So much of human history, however, is the story of people abusing their power to seek their own flourishing at the expense of others. We are a species bent toward injustice. When we misuse our power, we are not only inhibiting flourishing, and we are not only doing injustice to others, but we are also distorting the image of God we present.

Consider the power of a father over his child. Used properly, his power can create a home in which a child experiences love and protection. The father sets rules and boundaries for the child's safety and development, and he uses his strength for the best interests of his child, whom he loves. His power creates order so the child can flourish, and in this way the father reveals the image of God. Sadly, some fathers misuse their power by abusing their children in any number of ways—physically, emotionally, or even economically. In these cases the child will not flourish and is likely to develop distrust for all authority figures. Her ability to recognize the goodness of God will be severely impaired because the God-figure in her life did not reveal his image properly. Instead, she is presented with a false image of God—an idol of chaos and injustice bent on using her rather than blessing her. Injustice at its root is idolatry because it presents a false image of God to those being exploited.

This is the disordering that Sergeant Geiger is seeking to correct in Portland. Together with his special unit of officers, he is pursuing righteousness—the right ordering of relationships. The trafficked children, the pimps, the johns, and the entire city of Portland will flourish when the injustice of child prostitution is stopped. Sergeant Geiger is using his power to rightly order his part of the world, and in this way he is faithfully revealing the God whose image he carries.

## THE NEWS

Joslyn Baker is also on the front lines fighting Portland's child trafficking industry as a Commercial Sexual Exploitation of Children (CSEC) specialist with Multnomah County. "At the end of the day, we put the bad guy away and get the girl clothes and health treatment," she says. "But who loves her? Who tells her a story other than, 'The only thing you're good for is selling your body'?"[5]

Baker recognizes that seeking the right ordering of society is only part of our work as Christians in this world. Her specific calling is to help the government cultivate a more just and righteous community, but others in Portland are called by Christ to restore order in a different way. "When girls think they have no value to where they are selling themselves, something has been missed along the way," says Geiger. "This is something the church can do."

"The church has something special: We have the good news," says Shoshon Tama-Sweet, who has been working to end trafficking in Portland since 2005.[6]

Evangelism, or the sharing of the good news of Jesus Christ, is also part of cultivating order that leads to flourishing. Given the cantankerous debates being waged in the church today between advocates of social justice and evangelism, it may seem strange to view both callings as rooted in the same value. Those who believe in the priority of justice say that the church's evangelism will have no validity if not paired with social action. Christians who prioritize evangelism, however, argue that a person's eternal salvation must outweigh any temporal good he or she might achieve through social activism.

John Stott, having witnessed many of these battles, also wrestled with the question of evangelism or social justice, but he concluded that both sides of the controversy were in error. In his book *Christian Mission in the Modern World*, Stott argued that most people try to make social justice either superior or subordinate to evangelism.[7] The superior position diminishes the importance of calling people to be reconciled to God through Christ—something Stott found utterly incongruent with the New Testament. The subordinate position, however, he saw as equally untenable. It made social action into a public relations device, a way to win favor in order to spark more conversions. Stott wrote, "In its most blatant form this makes social work the sugar on the pill, the bait on the hook, while in its best forms it gives the gospel credibility it would otherwise lack. In either case the smell of hypocrisy hangs round our philanthropy."[8] Instead, Stott concluded that social justice and evangelism "belong to each other and yet are independent of each other. Each stands on its own feet in its own right alongside the other. Neither is a means to the other, or even a manifestation of the other. For each is an end in itself."[9]

What gets lost in the debates about evangelism and social justice, and what John Stott brings into sharper focus, is how both are part of God's work to cultivate order in the world. Restoring the proper order between God and people (evangelism) is an outworking of the gospel, but so is restoring a proper relationship between people within society (justice). When a person accepts the good news of the gospel, turns from his sin, and puts his faith in Christ, Paul said "his faith is courted as rightousness" in the sight of God.[10] In other words, he has a rightly ordered relationship with God unbroken by sin or rebellion. In this way, proclaiming the gospel is part of the Christian calling to cultivate order. By inviting others into life with God, we are working to restore the right ordering of the human-divine relationship, which leads to their flourishing. This is why churches are partnering with civil authorities in Portland against the trafficking of children. Those rescued from the streets need more than a bed, food, health care, and legal protection to flourish. They also need a sense of value and dignity that comes from knowing the love of God, their Maker.

When we understand evangelism to be part of God's right ordering of the world, it makes little sense to position it in opposition to social justice, but that appears to be what young Christians today are tempted to do. This may be a reaction to our culture's rapidly changing view of faith. As one young church leader told me, "When we speak of justice they love us. When we speak of Jesus they hate us." Ronald Sider, whose book *Rich Christians in an Age of Hunger* awakened a generation of evangelicals to the importance of justice, fears some followers of Christ are so eager to restore the importance of social activism in the church that they are ignoring the vital call to evangelism. Writing to young Christians, Sider said:

> You know how much I affirm your commitment to justice for the poor and your rejection of an evangelism that focuses only on the "soul" and neglects peoples' material needs. I have spent much of my life arguing on biblical grounds for precisely these concerns. But I have also watched some Christian "social activists" lose their concern for evangelism.[11]

While the temptation among many younger Christians is to emphasize social action over evangelism, the opposite temptation exists among many older Christians. In 2010, I attended the third Lausanne Congress for World Evangelization in Cape Town, South Africa. More than five thousand church leaders from around the globe gathered for the event, making it the largest, most diverse gathering of the church in world history. An American leader spoke to the delegates about the ongoing tension between evangelism and justice in the global church. He acknowledged not only the validity of alleviating human suffering in the present but also the need to reconcile people to God to avoid the eternal suffering of hell. He declared, "Could the global church say this: For Christ's sake we Christians care about all suffering, *especially* eternal suffering?"[12] While seeking to validate both justice and evangelism, the preacher fell into the same false dichotomy put forth by Eusebius in the fourth century. By emphasizing evangelism, or the avoidance of "eternal suffering," which the preacher called "ten million times worse than anything anybody will ever experience here," he diminished the value of working for justice upon the earth. Not only did his remarks ignore the fact that through Christ God is redeeming all things, including our physical bodies, and that Jesus' own ministry focused on the physical, material needs of those around him, this leader's remarks, like most debates about evangelism and social action, also lacked any discussion of *calling*.

If Christ calls me to the specific work of evangelism, then there can be no more important work for me to engage. Likewise, if he calls me to rescue children from the clutches of sex trafficking, that work should carry the greatest priority for my life. While many Christians seek to determine the value of evangelism or justice based on the outcome of each effort, a theology of vocation says each calling is valuable because of the One who calls us to it. John Stott, who happened to be a cofounder of the Lausanne Movement for World Evangelization, understood and affirmed this doctrine of specific calling. He said, "There is a diversity of Christian callings, and every Christian should be faithful to his own calling. The doctor must not neglect the practice of medicine for evangelism, nor should the evangelist be distracted from the ministry of the word by the ministry of tables, as the apostles quickly discovered [Acts 6]."[13]

Stott did not believe the calling of evangelism existed in tension with the work of social action. Each was a valid calling of Christ that should be celebrated within the church. If our goal is the establishment of shalom, the comprehensive flourishing of our world and those within it, then we cannot neglect evangelism as an essential part of restoring order. The garden city of God, if you recall, is the place not only where all injustice is made right but also where "the dwelling place of God is with man."[14] We cannot cultivate the order of Futureville without inviting people into a right relationship with God.

Likewise, if this world matters to God, and he is reconciling all things to himself through the power of the death and resurrection of Jesus, then pursuing the right ordering of this world through the establishment of justice is also important. Cultivating the righteousness of Futureville in the present both reveals the kingdom of God and points the world to the glorious and just future that is still to be revealed. So rather than viewing social justice and evangelism as existing in tension with each other, we ought to recognize them as two manifestations of the same characteristic of Futureville. They both seek the right ordering of the world for the flourishing of all, and how we engage each is not a matter of priority or guilt but one of calling.

The call to cultivate order is not limited to those seeking social justice or the proclamation of the gospel. We see it manifested in the pursuit of knowledge, the engineering of materials, and even in the most intimate and formative venue of human existence—the household. Jonathan Edwards once noted, "Family education and order are some of the chief means of grace; if these are duly maintained, all the means of grace are likely to prosper and become effectual."[15] That was certainly the case in my home as a child. My mother embodied the call to order both in her commitment to God and her instinct for justice. Like many nurturing Christian women, she cultivated a household in which knowledge of God was fostered through reading Bible stories before bed, in prayers, and through our participation in the church. She spoke openly about her faith and lived as if God was more than a theological idea or a superstition to be feared. Through her I received my first example of what a right relationship with God could be.

Her instinct for order, however, was not limited to the human-divine connection. She carried a strong sense of justice and fairness into everything she did. For example, she had a gift for finding the marginalized in any setting and making them feel treasured, and this wasn't merely fueled by her compassion. She knew there was something inherently wrong about a person not feeling valued and accepted. This led her to intentionally wait in the slowest checkout line at the supermarket where Michael, the mentally challenged man, bagged the groceries, just so she could talk to him, give him a hug, and encourage him. Michael always beamed when he saw my mother coming through his line. "Never treat a person differently just because they're not like you," she would tell me every time we left the store.

This sense of justice meant that bullying or teasing any disadvantaged person was an unforgivable sin in my mother's eyes. I could fail an exam or misbehave at school, but God help me if my mother ever discovered I had teased another kid, picked on a minority student, or participated in any form of bullying. I could see the fire in her eyes when someone in authority misused his power. In the face of injustice there was absolutely no chance she would remain passive. My brother and I witnessed her fearlessly confront school officials and intervene on behalf of an abused child; she once verbally eviscerated a dentist with a severe anger management problem in his waiting room. The event has come to be known in our family as simply "The Dr. Peterson Incident."

As people created in the image of God, we all carry an instinct to cultivate order. For those who live in communion with Christ, however, this call to order takes on new and varied dimensions. We see the impossibility of separating our pursuit of order with God from the pursuit of order in the world. As the fount of justice, when we live in unity with God, we cannot help but be channels for his ongoing ordering of the world. When this happens, as prophet Amos declared, we are participating in bringing closer the day when "justice [will] roll like waters, and righteousness like an ever-flowing stream."[16]

## THE TABLE

As the people of Christ—those made new by the power of his resurrection and the firstfruits of the new creation—the church is called to be a community that embodies the reality of the garden city of God in the present age. Throughout this chapter we have been exploring how the call to pursue justice (the right ordering of people with one another) is linked to our call to evangelize (the right ordering of people with God). These two manifestations of Futureville converge in the worship of the church. To understand how, we must first see the interplay between right worship and right relationships.

Throughout the Scriptures we find that having a properly ordered relationship to God is inseparable from having rightly ordered relationships among people. In Isaiah 1, God rejected the worship and festivals of his people because "everyone loves a bribe and runs after gifts. They do not bring justice to the fatherless, and the widow's cause does not come to them."[17] Later God told them what kind of worship he would accept:

*Is not this the fast that I choose:*
*to loose the bonds of wickedness,*
*to undo the straps of the yoke,*
*to let the oppressed go free,*
*and to break every yoke?*
*Is it not to share your bread with the hungry*
*and bring the homeless poor into your house;*
*when you see the naked, to cover him,*
*and not to hide yourself from your own flesh?*
*Then shall your light break forth like the dawn,*
*and your healing shall spring up speedily;*
*your righteousness shall go before you;*
*the glory of the* LORD *shall be your rear guard.*[18]

The link between our vertical relationship with God and our horizontal relationship with one another was also central to Jesus' teaching. He instructed us to be reconciled to our brother before we worship God,[19] and that failing to forgive others will prevent God from forgiving us.[20] Likewise, Paul said that through the cross Christ not only reconciled us to God by paying the price for our sins, but he also reconciled us to one another.[21] And John reminded us we cannot say we love God and not love each other.[22]

On this point the Bible is unequivocal—a correct ordering of the human-divine relationship necessitates the right ordering of all human relationships; we cannot separate our worship of God from our pursuit of justice. This message was true in the Old Testament through the prophets, and it was repeated in the New Testament by Jesus and his apostles. Reading Paul's first letter to the church in Corinth, we can feel the momentum of this biblical mandate as he instructs them about their worship gatherings. In 1 Corinthians 11, Paul rebuked the Corinthians for the "unworthy" manner in which they participated in the Lord's Supper. The problem was rooted in the unjust ordering of Corinthian society.

In Corinth, like most Greek and Roman cities, the rich and poor did not share meals together. Social stratification along economic lines was the norm, and the Christians of the city carried this ungodly value into their worship. Sunday, as noted in chapter 5, was not a day off from work in the ancient world. Therefore the poorer, working-class Christians gathered for worship later in the day after the wealthy believers had already enjoyed the Lord's Supper together, leaving only scraps. The Corinthians, both rich and poor, probably saw nothing wrong with this scenario, but the apostle Paul did:

> When you come together as a church, I hear that there are divisions among you. . . . When you come together, it is not the Lord's supper that you eat. For in eating, each one goes ahead with his own meal. One goes hungry, another gets drunk. What! Do you not have houses to eat and drink in? Or do you despise the church of God and humiliate those who have nothing?[23]

Paul blasted the Corinthians for their disunity in worship because he recognized that the Communion table was to represent the right ordering of the world. It was the symbol of the new creation inaugurated by the death and resurrection of Christ in which all things are made right. At the table we find the symbols through which our righteousness before God has been restored; by Christ's body and blood we may now live in right relationship to God. But his cross also reordered all human relationships. The injustices and divisions of race, gender, wealth, age, and class that scar our world were undone. Through the cross we have been made one. "There is neither Jew nor Greek, there is neither slave nor free, there is neither male nor female; for you are all one in Christ Jesus."[24] The Communion table looked forward to the coming day when all injustice would be made right in the garden city of God. The unity and fellowship experienced around the table was to be a foretaste, a preview of the new order in Futureville. The purpose of the table, therefore, was not merely to remember what Christ had done in the past, but also to remember the future.

Therefore, when the Corinthians exhibited the class divisions of their culture, they were "profaning the body and blood of the Lord"[25] and partaking in his table in "an unworthy manner."[26] Rather than revealing the new order of Christ, they were reflecting the old, broken order of the world. When the church understands the significance of the table correctly, however, Communion becomes a powerful vehicle for glimpsing Futureville and transporting it into the present. Christ's table displays to the cosmos collapsing under the fury of chaos and injustice what our God of order and righteousness is doing through the power of his gospel.

Bishop Desmond Tutu saw the new order of God displayed through the table during the terrible years of racial injustice that plagued his country. He wrote:

> As I have knelt in the Dean's stall at the superb 9.30 high mass, with incense, bells and everything, watching a multiracial crowd file up to the altar rails to be communicated, the one bread and one cup given by a mixed team of clergy and lay ministers with a multiracial choir, servers and sidemen—all this in apartheid-mad South Africa—the tears of joy sometimes streamed down my cheeks, tears of joy that it could be indeed that Jesus Christ had broken the wall of partition, that here were the first fruits of the eschatological community right in front of my eyes.[27]

The order of Futureville is cultivated not only through social action and evangelism, but also through the people of God gathered in unity and love around his table. There we display before the powers and agents of chaos in this world the new order inaugurated by Christ and carried forward by his people in anticipation of the day when the old order passes away and he makes all things new. At the table we manifest our righteousness with God through the body and blood of Jesus, and we reveal the justice of his kingdom as we heal all the divisions that have plagued our world since the rebellion in Eden.

In this chapter we have explored how God's people are called to establish order in a world marked by chaos. Through various callings, and in different patches of this planet, Christians are cultivating the order of Futureville so that God's will might be done on earth as it is in heaven. Order is cultivated when a pastor ministers at the Communion table and when a police officer takes down a ring of traffickers. Order is cultivated when a counselor cares for a victim of abuse and when a lost soul discovers the good news of Christ. Order is cultivated when a scientist categorizes a new species and when a politician signs a new law. Order is cultivated when a child constructs a tower of blocks and when humanity transforms a barren wilderness into a cultivated garden.

The value in each of these endeavors is not rooted in their outcomes but in obeying the Lord, who calls his servants to each one. This is his world, and he is in the process of making it new. As we work to bring order from chaos, his image is reflected in our joy.

# EIGHT
# BEAUTY

## THE TREES

"These beautiful things are here because God loves us," Harrison Higgins said as he walked through the forest. For Higgins the trees are more than raw material from which to manufacture furniture. They are gifts from God. "That means we handle them differently." Higgins uses eighteenth-century methods to handcraft beautiful chairs from raw lumber. Some resemble chairs designed three hundred years ago with talon feet and railed backs. Others are strikingly contemporary and would be at home in a museum of modern art. "You want the piece of furniture to measure up to the tree that it came from," Higgins says. That means carefully crafting each chair so that it will last hundreds of years. "We want what we build to be worth the life of the tree it came from."[1]

Harrison Higgins isn't merely a furniture maker. He is an artist. He recognizes the beauty God has instilled into creation. He admires and celebrates it as a gift from God, and then he uses it to craft even more beauty. The church is often confounded by Christians like Higgins. They simply don't know what to do with those called to the arts. Although many associate the historical church with some of the most celebrated artistic creations of Western civilization—Michelangelo's Sistine Chapel, Handel's *Messiah*, and Milton's *Paradise Lost* come to mind—many streams of Christianity have severely devalued the role of art in the present age. More practical concerns, like the right ordering of society, education, and the proclamation of the gospel, have pushed the arts to the sidelines. As a result, many artists feel their place within the church has been relegated to that of entertainers for the amusement of Christian consumers, but little more. What purpose could God possibly have for those, like Harrison Higgins, who are called to cultivate beauty in our world?

In the previous chapter we examined the human instinct to cultivate order and the various callings that reflect this aspect of God's character from the police officer to the evangelist. Order alone, however, cannot reflect the fullness of God or his image that we carry. We are also people who strive for splendor and the transcendent sense that comes from beholding the beautiful. Which other creatures of God, for example, are inspired by the brilliance of a starlit sky or are transported by rapturous music? Our desire for beauty, as well as our instinct to create it, are reflections of God's image in us. Long before Harrison Higgins admired the beauty of the trees, God himself was delighted by their appearance.

After cultivating order from the primordial chaos in Genesis 1, as we discovered in chapter 2, we then read that "the LORD God planted a garden in Eden, in the east, and there he put the man whom he had formed. And out of the ground the LORD God made to spring up every tree that is pleasant to the sight and good for food."[2] Biblical scholars have noted, and been confounded by, the fact that the beauty of the trees is expressed in these verses *before* their usefulness. Up to this point the creation narrative has been highly pragmatic. The ordering of time,[3] space,[4] and terrain[5] are all exceedingly practical endeavors. Even the creation of the garden as a suitable habitat for humans makes sense, as does the fruitfulness of the trees. But why emphasize the beauty of the trees? Unlike the other elements of the creation, the beauty of the trees serves no utilitarian function in the narrative.

The apostle Paul said the creation displays God's "invisible attributes, namely, his eternal power and divine nature."[6] The fact that the trees are not simply useful reveals that our God's attributes are not limited to the practical. He created the trees for their aesthetic value, for his own pleasure and to delight his image-bearers. The trees show a playfulness to God's character. As Harrison Higgins observed, the trees are a gift from God, and their beauty exists simply because he loves us. Beauty is an impractical extravagance that speaks of our God's own extravagant beauty and joyful character, and this desire to create and behold beauty is shared by those formed in his likeness.

## THE TENT

G. K. Chesterton was once asked what single book he would want if stranded on a desert island. "*Thomas' Guide to Practical Shipbuilding*," he answered.[7] Chesterton's supremely practical, and witty, answer reveals how a harsh environment can clarify one's priorities. The same was true for the Israelites while wandering in the wilderness of Sinai. They regularly grumbled to their leaders about their lack of food and water and even longed to return to slavery in Egypt rather than face death in the desert.

Amid the wilderness of Sinai the Lord proved his faithfulness and provided what his people needed in abundance (a quality we will cover in chapter 9)—meat and bread each morning and fresh water from rocks. He even ensured their clothing and shoes did not deteriorate on the journey. Surprisingly, however, God's provision went beyond their physical necessities. In the ugliness of Sinai he also ensured they had beauty. He gave Moses instructions to build an elaborate tent of worship. Known as the tabernacle, this portable house of worship was where the people would encounter God's presence and offer sacrifices. Constructed from the most precious materials, every surface of the tent was to be decorated with intricate patterns, symbols, and images—and the skills necessary to create this beautiful setting would come from God himself:

> The LORD has called by name Bezalel the son of Uri, son of Hur, of the tribe of Judah; and he has filled him with the Spirit of God, with skill, with intelligence, with knowledge, and with all craftsmanship, to devise artistic designs, to work in gold and silver and bronze, in cutting stones for setting, and in carving wood, for work in every skilled craft. And he has inspired him to teach, both him and Oholiab the son of Ahisamach of the tribe of Dan. He has filled them with skill to do every sort of work done by an engraver or by a designer or by an embroiderer in blue and purple and scarlet yarns and fine twined linen, or by a weaver—by any sort of workman or skilled designer.[8]

If stranded in the desert, I could think of more practical skills to request from God than embroidery and graphic design, but God was not content for his people merely to survive in the wilderness. He wanted them to thrive. The creation of the tabernacle, as well as the empowering of individuals with artistic skills, reveals God's intent for beauty to mark his presence and the presence of his people. While wandering in the desert, the Israelites did not need a beautiful tabernacle; a simpler, less decorative one would have done the job. A more austere tent, however, would not have reflected the beauty of the God they worshipped there, nor would it have provided his people with the beauty their spirits longed for in that dry and desolate place.

God calls some people today, like Oholiab and Bezalel in ages past, to create beauty. Their calling is not entirely practical, but it is important. Through their work they reflect the beauty of God and reveal an important aspect of his character. Even those of us called to other vocations can participate in the cultivation of beauty and be drawn closer to God through it. Although my father's calling was to medicine, his love for music and gardening showed his appreciation for beauty. He was skeptical of the church and what he called "organized religion." (I've told him if he engaged the church more often, he'd realize we're not that organized.) On Sunday mornings, when my mom was wrangling us off to church, my father would be in the sunroom watering his plants and sipping his tea. In the summer months he would walk barefoot through his flower beds picking weeds and admiring the fruits of his labor. "This is my church," he told me once while in his garden. "This is where I see God."

My father was responsible for helping me appreciate the arts. He filled our home with music—everything from Beethoven to Victor Borge to the Beatles. He was always playing, or learning to play, some instrument—piano, saxophone, harmonium, Indian tabla—and he worked tirelessly to develop his singing voice. When my own musical talent failed to blossom, he encouraged me toward the visual arts with community art classes and books on drawing and painting. His appreciation for beauty was evident even in his vocation as a doctor. He loved the art, and not just the science, of medicine. The beautiful efficiency of human anatomy and the skill of a well-sutured laceration brought him joy. When my daughter fell and required stitches on her forehead, I called my father on our way to the emergency room. "Don't let those butchers touch my granddaughter!" he barked. This was a case requiring the touch of an artist, not just the skill of a doctor. He called a plastic surgeon to ensure the beauty of his granddaughter's face was not overlooked in the process of healing her wound.

My father understood that there was more to life than medicine, and more to medicine than health. Although he chafed against the abuses of dogmatic religion, he recognized that the arts pointed to God and that atheism could not account for the infinite layers of beauty evident in the world. Earlier I quoted G. K. Chesterton's practical answer to the imaginary scenario of being stranded on an island, but Chesterton also validated the importance of beauty. Responding to the rise of atheism in his day, Chesterton argued that advocates of atheism had no way of valuing the impractical. He wrote:

> Then there is what there always is in such philosophy, the setting of the cart to draw the horse. They do not see that digestion exists for health, and health exists for life, and life exists for the love of music or beautiful things. They reverse the process and say that the love of music is good for the process of digestion. What the process of digestion is ultimately good for they have really no idea. I think it was a great mediaeval philosopher who said that all evil comes from enjoying what we ought to use and using what we ought to enjoy. A great many modern philosophers never do anything else.[9]

Chesterton's critique applies equally today, and not just to atheism. A great deal of Christianity has also lost the ability to value the impractical and the beautiful. This aspect of God's character and his creation is increasingly pushed aside by the overwhelming practicality of our consumer culture. Rather than seeing the Creator as a beautiful God to be worshipped, many churches sell Jesus like he is a duct tape/WD-40 combo pack—all you need to fix just about anything. We praise him as the Almighty Improver and the means by which our dreams and goals can be achieved. As a result, our worship often carries a hidden, exceedingly practical agenda. We believe that our praise and sacrifices will obligate God to act on our behalf.

This transactional vision of worship was on display a few years ago when a wide receiver for a professional football team dropped a pass in the end zone. After the game he blamed God for the loss via Twitter. "I praise you 24/7!!! And this is how you do me!!! You expect me to learn from this???How??? I'll never forget this!! Ever!!"[10] The athlete viewed his worship as a tool for manipulating God; in his mind worship was a transaction that served a practical purpose. In exchange for his devotion, God was supposed to help him on the football field. This approach does not value God as someone to worship but as something to use. He is a means to an end.

This is what happens when we lose sight of beauty, when we succumb to the utilitarian inclinations of our sinful hearts and commercial culture. Without the impracticality of beauty, we miss the truth that some things exist simply to behold and not to be used; we have no way of recognizing the inherent and infinite value of God himself. This fact helps us understand why God wanted the tabernacle to be a place of impractical beauty, and not just a useful tent of worship. *Worship* means "to ascribe worth." It sees the intrinsic, rather than the transactional, value of that which is being praised. Unlike religions fueled by superstition, divination, or fear, true Christian faith does not worship God with a utilitarian goal in mind. It is not transactional. It is not useful. Worship is an impractical and beautiful act of adoration that flows from a heart transfixed by the beauty of God. True worship cares for nothing in return but the presence of God himself, as David sings in Psalm 27:

> *One thing have I asked of the Lord,*
> *that will I seek after:*
> *that I may dwell in the house of the Lord*
> *all the days of my life,*
> *to gaze upon the beauty of the Lord.*[11]

## THE USELESS

The unparalleled beauty of God, and his care to cultivate beauty both at the beginning of creation and again in the wilderness of Sinai, is why the church, above all, should affirm the vocation of artists. Their calling reminds us that not everything in the cosmos was created to be used and that beauty has an important, nonutilitarian function in our world. Beauty is not listed among air, food, and water on Maslow's hierarchy of needs, but we must remember that the word *shalom* is concerned not merely with human survival but with human flourishing. This is why beauty is an integral part of God's perfect world from the start. His intent was not merely for his image-bearers to get by. He desired for us to thrive and flourish—to delight in the wonder, awe, and joy of a world filled with reflections of his beauty.

Environmental psychologists have documented that people will often devote themselves to creative and aesthetic projects even when their basic physical needs are not satisfied.[12] They have found that people without enough to eat will still expend energy to grow flowers. Researchers report these small glimpses of beauty offer a sense of tranquility and even transcendence. It fills the person with hope amid horrible circumstances. Beauty feeds an aspect of the human spirit that food alone cannot nourish. Similarly, a landmark study by Roger Ulrich in 1984 found that patients recovering from surgery in the hospital with a view of a tree recovered faster, required less pain medicine, and had fewer infections than patients with only a view of a brick wall.[13] The research confirms what we know from Scripture: humans deprived of beauty may survive, but they cannot thrive.

Beauty and order are not opposed to each other even if one is supremely practical and the other is not. Writing requires ordering words, and music requires ordering notes, but when our writing or playing is pursued with the goal of creating something beautiful we move beyond the practical. We engage an aspect of God's image that is unique to humanity. We become artists. Andy Crouch says, "Art is one way of naming everything we as cultural beings do that cannot be explained in terms of its usefulness."[14]

This may be the reason those called by God to artistic vocations have found the church a challenging community in which to pursue their callings. The mandate to cultivate beauty in the world does not always submit to the practical works championed within the church. As a result, to find acceptance by the church, let alone affirmation, many artists feel their creations must carry an explicitly Christian message. It isn't enough to compose a beautiful song—it must be a Christian song. It isn't acceptable to create an inspiring film—it must have an evangelistic message. It isn't sufficient to write a brilliant novel—it must champion biblical values. For many Christians, beauty is only to be valued when it can be utilized for some practical purpose, which explains the dreadfully uninspiring architecture of most evangelical churches. When creativity is forced to submit to practicality, however, it quickly leaves the realm of art and moves closer to the dangerous territory of propaganda.

In this regard the contemporary church has something in common with the Soviet Union. In her book about the Soviet domination of Eastern Europe, *Iron Curtain*, Anne Applebaum notes why the Soviets feared abstract art. "Art was supposed to tell a story. It was supposed to teach. It was supposed to support the ideals of the party," Applebaum explained in an interview. Abstract art was open to interpretation and carried no discernible message. This was simply unacceptable to Alexander Dymschitz, head of the cultural division of the Soviet Military

Administration, who said, "Form without content means nothing." Therefore the Soviets went to great lengths to display only art, music, and architecture that conveyed a clear message. "There was no such thing as art for art's sake," said Applebaum. "There was no such thing as art reaching into a spiritual or wordless realm."[15] To the Soviets beauty had no inherent value, only order. Their order.

The Soviets insisted that beauty submit to practicality. Their worldview had no capacity to value anything or anyone that did not advance its agenda—a fact manifested in the murder of millions of people by communist regimes. When beauty is demoted on the hierarchy of human flourishing, we become increasingly incapable of valuing anything apart from its utilitarian function. All things and all people become subject to the brutal evaluation of usefulness.

The Christian worldview stands in unwavering opposition to all forms of utilitarianism. Our faith affirms the God-given value of every person regardless of their usefulness—a belief increasingly challenged in a world driven by the practicalities of commerce, a world that still enslaves 27 million people and aborts 44 million children every year. Yes, God has organized his world to be useful, but he has also imbued it with the impractical quality of beauty to remind us that value is not defined by usefulness. Not all things exist to be used. Some things exist simply to be adored.

Along with the inherent value of God and people, the uselessness of beauty also helps us grasp the nature of God's grace. Daniel Siedell wrote:

> Art is about discontinuity and contradiction, which is how grace is experienced in the world, as an alien intrusion into a world that deceives us into believing that we are defined by what we do, not by what Christ has done. And so we are compelled to prove ourselves, to make something that justifies our existence. But art is not just doing and making, it is also receiving, and hearing. It is not just an achievement; it is a gift. It is devoting one's life to something so futile, inefficient, and in many ways useless, that it becomes a means of grace.[16]

The graceful, useless nature of beauty was revealed in an event shortly before Jesus' death. While reclining at a table, a woman poured an expensive flask of ointment on his feet. When his disciples saw this, they were appalled. Like many religious people today, they could only see through the lens of practicality. "This ointment could have been sold for more than three hundred denarii and given to the poor," they said, rebuking the woman.

"Leave her alone," Jesus shot back at them. "Why do you trouble her? She has done a beautiful thing to me."[17]

For those who believe the beautiful must submit to the practical, it is impossible to view the woman's action as anything but wasteful. The disciples saw the spilled ointment as a lost opportunity. To them the ointment was only a commodity to be utilized and exchanged for a measurable outcome; therefore, pouring it onto the floor was a waste. What they interpreted as a waste, however, Jesus saw as priceless. He recognized the spilled ointment as beautiful, impractical worship. True worship can never be wasteful because it seeks nothing in return. It carries no transaction. True worship is always a gift.

Beauty exists for no practical reason. It is a gift from God that delights and inspires us, and so are those called by God to cultivate beauty in our world and in the church. Their vocations remind us that the most precious things are often the least useful. Through their vocations, artists provoke to see the world differently—not simply as a bundle of resources to be used, but as a gift to be received. Therefore, the creative arts serve as a model of God's grace, and how the church affirms and celebrates the vocations of artists is likely to impact its vision of God. As Crouch said, "If we have a utilitarian attitude toward art, if we require it to justify itself in terms of its usefulness to our ends, it is very likely that we will end up with the same attitude toward worship, and ultimately toward God."[18] To those in the church who cannot affirm the calling of artists, who insist creativity must submit to practicality, perhaps Jesus would say, "Why do you bother them? They are doing beautiful things for me."

## THE DEFIANT

On May 28, 1992, the principal cellist in the Sarajevo opera dressed in his formal black tails and sat down on a fire-scorched chair in a bomb crater to play Albinoni's *Adagio in G Minor.* The site was outside a bakery in Smajlović's neighborhood where twenty-two people waiting in line for bread had been killed the previous day. During the siege of Sarajevo from 1992 to 1995, more than ten thousand people were killed. The citizens lived in constant fear of shelling and snipers while struggling each day to find food and water. Smajlović lived near one of the few working bakeries where a long line of people had been gathered when a shell exploded. He rushed to the scene and was overcome with grief at the carnage. For the next twenty-two days, one for each victim of the bombing, he decided to challenge the ugliness of war with his only weapon—beauty.

Known as the "Cellist of Sarajevo," Smajlović not only performed outside the bakery but continued to unleash the beauty of his music in graveyards, at funerals, in the rubble of buildings, and in the sniper-infested streets. "I never stopped playing music throughout the siege," he said. "My weapon was my cello." Although completely vulnerable, Smajlović was never shot. It was as if the beauty of his presence repelled the violence of war. His music created an oasis amid the horror. It offered hope to the people of Sarajevo and a vision of beauty to the soldiers who were destroying the city. A reporter asked him if he was crazy for playing in a war zone. Smajlović replied, "Why do you not ask if they are crazy for shelling Sarajevo?"[19]

Smajlović's story shows another aspect of the artist's calling. Vocations that cultivate beauty not only reveal God's character and teach us to value the impractical, but they also defy the sinfulness of our world. Christian artists stand in prophetic defiance to all that is wicked and ugly, and through their works they offer us a window to the world that is to come.

Winston Churchill observed, "War is the normal occupation of man. War—and gardening."[20] His statement captures the paradoxical truth of our human condition. We are bent on destruction, yet we long for beauty. In war we see the ultimate expression of our utilitarianism. War is the willingness to sacrifice everything to achieve a goal. When the tanks of war roll, everything is crushed beneath their treads, leaving only ugliness behind. Gardening, however, is the opposite of war. It is an act of creation rather than destruction, order rather than chaos, and beauty rather than ugliness. By playing his cello in the center of war-torn Sarajevo, Smajlović was planting a garden amid the battlefield. He was confronting the sinfulness of man, seen in the horrible practicality of war, with the beauty of God, seen in the extravagant impracticality of art.

Art is more than a luxury, and beauty is more than a frill. When we create art and music, or when we gather to worship with expressions of splendor and adoration, like Smajlović we are performing an act of defiance. We are creating an oasis of beauty amid the onslaught of ugliness. We are declaring our refusal to succumb to the brokenness of the world and instead looking forward to a Futureville where all things will radiate the beauty of the Creator. These acts of defiance, however, are not strictly practical. In fact, their power is often found precisely in their impracticality. George Eisen, in his book *Children and Play in the Holocaust*, examined the way children defied the Nazis in World War II. On the surface their games appeared to be little more than distractions or a childish use of time, but Eisen concluded that children's play in the concentration camps and ghettos was actually "an enterprise of survival, a defense of sanity and a demonstration of psychological defiance."[21] Children could not overcome the soldiers with weapons or strength, so instead they resisted them with smiles and laughter.

Similarly, when Christians participate in the arts or are called into vocations of beauty, they may be accused of devoting themselves to impractical pursuits—including by some within the church. "Shouldn't they be seeking to influence the world and overcome evil through the practical channels of commerce, government, and education?" critics may ask. "And wouldn't the efforts of the church be better served through church planting or evangelism?" For Christians called by God into those vocations that is certainly an appropriate thing, but their callings do not negate the value of the artist's. The Christian artist is engaged in a subtle but powerful defiance of her own. She is playfully refusing to submit to the ugliness of the world, and in her cultivation of beauty she is creating an oasis for others fleeing the darkness.

The desire to create an oasis of beauty led Troy and Sara Groves to purchase an old church building and open Art House North in Saint Paul, Minnesota. The Groves have spent most of the last fourteen years on tour as musicians, but they had a growing desire to do something to foster creativity in their own city. Art House North is a hub for Christians called into artistic vocations to support one another and display their works to inspire the community of Saint Paul. Troy Groves said part of the motivation for the project came while touring in Washington, DC. They were invited to a lunch with government leaders in the Senate dining room. "They sat us down and said, 'You know, after a career of working on Capitol Hill, we've come to realize that in politics, we're just responding to culture. But it's the artists who are creating it—for good, or for bad.' In what ways were we wielding this power of art in our city, and in our different spheres of influence?"[22]

The Groves are using Art House North to foster "a creative culture for the common good." They recognize it isn't just the practical vocations, like politics, that are used by God to combat evil and achieve his purposes in the world, but also the impractical callings of artists. They see artists, musicians, and storytellers as having a formative and preservative effect upon a community. They are creating a space both to incubate and curate their works for the benefit of everyone in the city, and through their art they cultivate hope amid the often ugly realities of urban life. Yes, those living in urban centers need safe neighborhoods, well-resourced schools, and access to jobs, but even more foundational to these practical needs is hope. Without hope no amount of practical assistance will be effective. Art House North is a beacon of hope in Saint Paul just as Smajlović's cello was in war-torn Sarajevo.

The power of hope through beauty was seen in London in 2009 when the National Gallery held an exhibition of seventeenth-century Spanish art called "The Sacred Made Real." The display featured paintings and sculptures of the suffering of Jesus, the Virgin Mary, and the saints in vivid realism. Many feared the religious art would go unappreciated by the highly secular culture of London. That was not the case. Roberta Ahmanson, a sponsor of the exhibit, recalled a woman meditating before Pedro de Mena's *Virgin of Sorrows*. "The woman's gaze was not a blank stare. No, something was going on inside her, something private."[23]

Adirian Searle, writing for a London newspaper, said about the exhibit, "There is so much more to say and think about here, whatever one believes, or whatever belief one feels estranged from. Painted or sculpted, these are real presences. I left devastated and deeply moved." The museum hoped for thirty-five thousand visitors. More than ninety thousand came. "Beauty drew them; it gave them hope," said Ahmanson.[24]

Some will look at the efforts of Vedran Smajlović, Troy and Sara Groves, and Roberta Ahmason and argue that there are more practical ways to help our world. No doubt there are, and God has called some of his people to engage those tasks. But in the face of war, poverty, failing schools, social decay, hunger, injustice, and emotional trauma, there is also a place for the defiant work of artists. They articulate our pain while pointing us toward a hope beyond the present darkness. Their vocations provides us a glimpse of a world still being born where God will "wipe away every tear from their eyes, and death shall be no more, neither shall there be mourning, nor crying, nor pain anymore."[25]

The defiant calling of the artist to cultivate hope was articulated by a community of artists in the 1930s. Their words might apply equally to Christians called by God to cultivate Futureville today. Meeting in Europe under the growing shadow of war, they would say to one another, "How can one think about planting roses when the forests are burning?" To which they responded, "How can you not plant roses when the forests are burning?"[26]

NINE

# ABUNDANCE

## THE BUBBLE

Walter Crutchfield's family has been developing real estate in Arizona since 1952. "The last real estate cycle was unlike anything I've ever seen before," he recalled. New homes were being built at a dizzying pace as neighborhoods and gated communities were being planned up to sixty miles outside of Phoenix. "You felt that if you didn't move quickly you were going to be left out." In order to keep the real estate market growing, Walter said, mortgages were being given to people who had no way of paying them. "We were servicing demand without asking if it was sustainable."[1] This rapid growth was built on a foundation of greed and debt, and eventually the bubble burst.

The recent real estate boom and bust in the United States,

along with the global economic recession that followed, was fueled by a powerful fear driving many people—scarcity. In Eden the man and woman enjoyed an abundance of what they needed to live. In the garden God had caused to grow every tree that was good for food, and he provided abundant water and resources; outside the garden, in the wilderness, humans had to toil and strive to acquire food, shelter, and provisions. We now occupy a world where we live with the constant fear of not having enough, so when we encounter bounty our instinct is to hoard—to gather as much for ourselves as possible. In Walter Crutchfield's case, fear of scarcity caused him and many other real estate developers to race after more and more land, and it caused banks to issue ever riskier loans.

Walter discovered the blinding effect of fear. Frantically grasping for more causes us to lose sight of everything outside of ourselves. Thomas Aquinas equated this kind of fear with a "contraction" of the soul. It is a force that pulls us inward. This impulse, said Aquinas, begins in the imagination. When we encounter a powerful force outside ourselves, our imaginations label it a "threatening evil which is difficult to repel."[2] We respond by taking a defensive, contracted posture, drawing our strength inward. Imagine a city under siege. The forces of the enemy are assailing it on every side, so the inhabitants flee the countryside, retreat behind the city's walls, close the gates, and barricade themselves within the central quarters. They contract in fear to protect the limited resources they have. This explains the blindness of real estate developers during the land rush around Phoenix. While feverishly securing their own financial futures, they were unable to see the harm being inflicted by their actions or the eventual collapse that was to come. Only after the bubble burst did they see the truth. "The real estate crash brought me to a place of stepping back and evaluating," said Walter. "I realized I had lost sight of the value of individuals, of work, and of the community." Greed fueled by fear makes us incapable of seeing beyond ourselves.

Unlike Aquinas's self-centered and contracted city, Futureville is not ruled by the fear of scarcity but by the blessing of abundance. In John's Revelation, we are told that the gates of the garden city are never shut.[3] In other words, there is no threat that would ever cause the inhabitants of Futureville to retreat behind walls or gates. There is no fear of scarcity that would cause its citizens to contract inward and hoard their resources. Instead, citizens of Futureville are able to live expanding lives that look ever upward and outward. They can see the world through eyes of faith rather than fixate upon themselves with eyes of fear.

Throughout the Bible we see this tension between fear and faith, between scarcity and abundance. In the exodus story, Pharaoh represents the way of the world as he seeks safety through control and acquisition. He creates great storehouses of grain and wealth, he uses armies to take over land, and he enslaves the Hebrews to provide labor for his empire. When Pharaoh fears the Hebrews are growing too numerous and might threaten his power, he orders their children thrown into the Nile and killed.

Egypt was a kingdom ruled by fear, which led to immense evil, and the same pattern can be seen in modern societies. In 1933, Martin Niemöller was a young pastor in Germany and part of a delegation of church leaders invited to a meeting with Adolf Hitler. He silently observed the new German chancellor from the back of the room. Later Niemöller's wife asked him what he had learned in the meeting. "I discovered that Herr Hitler is a terribly frightened man," he replied.[4] Scarcity makes us afraid, our fear causes us to seek control, and our striving for control can lead to unimaginable evil.

In contrast to the gated kingdoms of the world driven by the fear of scarcity, the kingdom of God is marked by the faith of abundance. Its gates are never shut. When the Lord led his people out of Egypt into the wilderness, the people feared not having enough food and water, but each day God provided what they needed. Quail fell over the camp every evening for meat, and bread from heaven covered the ground every morning. God's people always had enough. Those who tried to hoard the manna discovered that whatever they kept from the previous day rotted overnight. Unlike the kings of the world who are driven by fear to hoard and acquire, the Lord was teaching his people the truth that control is an illusion, and rather than seeking control they were to surrender in faith and trust in his abundant provision each day.[5] Faith rather than fear marks his kingdom.

We see this quality of Futureville in Jesus' ministry. On numerous occasions those gathered to hear him did not have enough to eat. Giving thanks to God, Jesus took a few fish and loaves of bread and fed thousands. Not only was there always enough, but the disciples managed to gather an abundance of leftovers. These miraculous feedings were signs that the kingdom of God had arrived, that scarcity would be no more, and that Futureville had broken into the world with Jesus. The gate to the garden of abundance had been opened again.

Centuries earlier Isaiah had prophesied that abundance would accompany the Messiah's coming:

*Come, everyone who thirsts,*
*come to the waters;*
*and he who has no money,*
*come, buy and eat!*
*Come, buy wine and milk*
*without money and without price.*[6]

John echoed Isaiah's words when concluding his description of the garden city: "The Spirit and the Bride say, 'Come.' And let the one who hears say, 'Come.' And let the one who is thirsty come; let the one who desires take the water of life without price."[7]

The message of Scripture is unwavering—with God there is always enough. Where he reigns, we never have to fear scarcity. We do not have to retreat in fear behind a locked gate or scramble to get as much as we can before the market tumbles. In his kingdom of abundance the gates are never shut; bubbles never form or bust. Our captivity to sin and fear can often cause us to lose sight of this remarkable truth. As Walter

Brueggemann recognized, "We must confess that the central problem of our lives is that we are torn apart by the conflict between our attraction to the good news of God's abundance and the power of our belief in scarcity—a belief that makes us greedy, mean and unneighborly."[8]

The real estate crash caused Walter Crutchfield to acknowledge this conflict in his own life. He had lost sight of God's abundance, and the fear of scarcity had caused him to ignore the needs of his neighbors. Today, rather than chasing after more profit in unsustainable ways or developing land unreflectively, he is using his business skills to seek the flourishing of his city. Walter and his partners now target poor, under-resourced neighborhoods to bring revitalization. "We took a number of buildings on the corner of Seventh and McDowell that were really decrepit," he reports. "We preserved what was historic and beautiful in those buildings, and we created a new purpose for them."[9] Retailers and restaurants now occupy the corner, providing services and jobs to a part of Phoenix that desperately needed them. The open courtyard filled with flowers and tables has become a safe community gathering place. A lot once marked by decay, ugliness, and scarcity has been transformed into an oasis of order, beauty, and abundance.

Walter has attempted similar projects in other parts of Phoenix to ensure poorer neighborhoods have access to affordable groceries. He has used market competition to pressure convenience stores to stop selling liquor in areas where drug abuse and alcoholism is rampant, and the profit he generates from these developments is not hoarded for his own enjoyment and security but reinvested to cultivate growth in other struggling neighborhoods. Faith in God's abundance, rather than fear over the world's scarcity, has freed Walter to use his calling to seek the shalom of his city.

## THE MARKETPLACE

We have already seen that God has called some of his people to cultivate order in the world and others, beauty; we can see how these qualities are imbued with Christian significance. We have a more difficult time, however, recognizing the divine vocation to cultivate abundance, because many with this call pursue it through the marketplace—a realm historically ignored or demonized by much of the church. Walter Crutchfield retained a joy for business after becoming a Christian. He explained to me, "But those around me said that business was something less, and that if I was serious about my faith, I'd need to get involved in the church and ministry." He said Christians in business are told to take the gospel with them to work and to treat others fairly, but the church never directly validates their work in the marketplace. Another successful businessman once confided to me that "in the body of Christ I feel like I am only the back pocket." Church leaders valued him for his capacity to fund ministries, but they never recognized the way his vocation created jobs, transformed communities, or elevated households out of poverty.

Amy Sherman, in research she conducted for her book

*Kingdom Calling*, confirmed that the message Walter heard from the church is not uncommon. Looking at workplace ministries over the last century, Sherman said most have focused on the "three Es"—ethics, evangelism, and excellence. "Being people of good character, witnessing to our co-workers, and doing our work with excellence are all important parts of integrating faith and work," she said. "But there is much more to be said beyond the three Es. When we begin to understand this invitation from Jesus to join his mission of restoring all things, our enthusiasm for integrating faith and work will be heightened."[10]

No doubt the church's struggle to affirm the marketplace and its role in God's plan to cultivate abundance stems in part from the rampant abuses and greed associated with the business world. The global economic meltdown of 2008 was linked to systemic corruption at a number of the world's largest banks. Goldman Sachs, for example, lied to regulators about the scale of Greece's national debt, resulting in the collapse of banks throughout Europe, and Goldman was fined $550 million by the US Securities and Exchange Commission for misleading its own clients in order to accumulate more profit for itself. When confronted by a reporter about these scandals and his firm's role in the global recession, Goldman's CEO, Lloyd Blankfein, said he was simply "doing God's work."[11] The remark enraged many who lost their jobs, homes, and savings in the collapse while the bankers responsible were issued $27-million bonuses. Blankfein justified the bonuses by saying, "We're very important. We help companies to grow by helping them to raise capital. Companies that grow create wealth. This, in turn, allows people to have jobs that create more growth and more wealth. We have a social purpose."[12]

Blankfein's comments reveal that even a broken watch is right twice a day. Indeed, bankers do have a social purpose, and those called by God into the marketplace are doing his work. They help create an abundance of jobs, opportunity, homes, food, and many other essential resources for life and flourishing; when the marketplace and government work properly, more of the world's people discover the blessing of having enough. Research by the World Bank has found that the number of people in the world living on less than $1.25 per day (the most commonly accepted poverty line) has been reduced by half since 1990, and for the first time poverty rates are declining in every region of the globe. Most of this decline is attributed to economic growth in previously impoverished countries fueled by open markets with thoughtful government regulation. As Walter Crutchfield discovered in Phoenix, when business is pursued for the common good rather than individual greed, entire communities can flourish.

However, the opposite is also true. When greed and fear drive those in the marketplace or government, the abundance produced often benefits only the few holding the reins of power. This is why so many view the global investment banks with contempt, and it is the most significant factor keeping millions imprisoned in poverty around the world. Mehul Srivastava asked why India, a country with abundant, fertile land, cannot feed all its people, and why Indians are consuming fewer calories today than in the 1980s despite having one of the fastest-growing economies in the world. He found the root of India's malnutrition is not a lack of food but rather "corruption, incompetence, and official indifference." Srivastava documents how "record stockpiles of grain rot in warehouses, and supplies meant for the poor are often stolen. As much as $14.5 billion worth of food in one conspiracy was looted by corrupt politicians over 10 years from my father's state of Uttar Pradesh alone, according to court documents." The World Bank found that India spends $14 billion a year to help feed its poorest citizens, but nearly 40 percent of that aid is stolen or mishandled.[13]

This is why the Christian's presence in both the marketplace and public sector is essential, and why the church must affirm and equip more people to manifest the values of Futureville in these channels. The temptation of wealth and power is so strong that without a sense of God's calling, Christians can easily fall into the same greed that infects many others in business and government. By remaining silent about the call to cultivate abundance for the sake of others, the church is abandoning these critical functions of God's world to the forces of idolatry and materialism. Dorothy Sayers saw this danger:

> In nothing has the Church so lost Her hold on reality as in Her failure to understand and respect the secular vocation. She has allowed work and religion to become separate departments, and is astonished to find that, as result, the secular work of the world is turned to purely selfish and destructive ends.[14]

A remarkable recalibration is possible, however, when Christians enter the marketplace with a sense of divine responsibility and Christian virtue. Proverbs says, "When the righteous prosper, the city rejoices."[15] The righteous, as we learned in chapter 7, are those with a rightly ordered relationship to God and others. When these humble, justice-seeking servants of God prosper, they do not hoard their wealth or selfishly seek their own comfort at the expense of others. Instead, the entire community can rejoice at their successes because the righteous will use their power, wealth, and influences to bless others. They will steward their abundance in a manner that cultivates shalom—comprehensive flourishing—for everyone in the community.

## THE PLATE

Affirming and equipping those called into the marketplace or the government is a critical responsibility if the church is to offer glimpses of Futureville to our broken world—but it is not the church's only responsibility. In Ephesians 4:28, Paul reminds us that abundance is not cultivated merely through our work, but also by sharing the fruit of that work. "Let the thief no longer steal, but rather let him labor, doing honest work with his own hands, so that he may have something to share with anyone in need." Paul's logic here is surprising. He not only contrasts the way a person acquires his daily bread—dishonest stealing versus honest labor—but he also contrasts why a thief steals and a Christian works. Paul implies that the thief uses what he acquires only for himself, but the Christian works with the goal of providing for others. Work is more than a way of overcoming the scarcity of the world for ourselves. When linked with generosity, it becomes a means of cultivating abundance for everyone.

Christ calls many of his servants to vocations that cultivate abundance. The farmer, the grocer, the factory worker, the salesman, the business owner, the banker, the marketer, the real estate developer, and countless others engage in honest work that produces more of what we all need to live. When these tasks are undertaken for the common good, they bring flourishing, but Paul's words in Ephesians remind us that abundance is also cultivated through generosity. When we ignore giving as part of God's plan for creating abundance, we can fall into the trap of what President George H. W. Bush famously called "voodoo economics"—the belief that assisting the poor through charity or government is unnecessary because the economic activities of the rich will, in time, trickle down to benefit the poor through the invisible hand of the market. This belief was why Gordon Gekko, the notorious investment banker in the film *Wall Street*, could declare, "Greed is good." His twisted logic concluded that seeking only his self-interest would eventually and indirectly help the poor.

In the Christian worldview, however, greed is never good. Rather than a passive approach to assisting the poor, Paul calls us to share directly with those in need. For many Christians this way of cultivating abundance is often on display during worship gatherings. In the preceding chapters we saw how both order and beauty are manifested in worship. At the Communion table we display the right ordering of both human and divine relationships, and through the arts we reflect the beauty of God when we assemble. Likewise, the value of abundance in God's kingdom is manifested when money is collected to provide for the poor and needy in our midst. As the offering plate is passed to the worker, farmer, and banker, they are confronted with the truth that providing for the needs of others cannot be limited to their efforts in the marketplace; abundance must also be cultivated through the sacrifice of sharing.

Many are uncomfortable with the collection of money in worship—particularly those outside Christian communities who find the mingling of dollars and deities unseemly. As already noted, there exists within the church a view that finances are inherently earthly and should be confined to the more profane spheres of commerce and business, while the church should occupy itself with the things of heaven. Adding to our discomfort is the perception that offerings are used to line the pockets of church leaders or feed their egos through institutional expansion rather than to feed the poor or shelter the homeless. The abuse of money by religious institutions and leaders is nauseatingly common, but this does not negate the importance of financial giving as an element of Christian devotion. If the gathering of the church is to offer a glimpse of Futureville—to showcase order, beauty, and abundance to a world shattered by chaos, ugliness, and scarcity—then sharing our resources with those who have less must be part of our worship. To ignore this quality of Futureville would leave one of the world's greatest injustices unchallenged and uncorrected.

For this reason a commitment to sharing has been evident in Christian communities since the beginning. Earlier we looked at the miraculous feedings performed by Jesus. Thousands were provided an abundance of fish and bread as a sign that the messianic kingdom had arrived. The same miracle occurs again within the early church, although the miracle is easily overlooked. In Acts 2, and again in Acts 4, we read that the believers with money, possessions, and land shared what they had to ensure "there was not a needy person among them."[16] No one lacked food, clothing, or a place to lay his or her head. Everyone had enough. Unlike Jesus' feeding of the crowds, scarcity was not the challenge to be overcome. Enough resources existed to satisfy everyone's needs, but the resources were not equally accessible. The miracle in Acts was not the physical multiplication of food, but the spiritual transformation of hearts. The Christians were filled with such love and generosity that they joyfully shared their abundance with their neighbors. Faith in God's provision had overcome their fear of scarcity. Giving triumphed over greed.

Paul later made the same appeal to the Christians in Corinth when a famine threatened the church in Jerusalem. He invited the Corinthians to give out of their abundance to aid those in scarcity so "that there may be fairness."[17] He concluded his request by quoting from Exodus 16, the story of God's people receiving manna in the wilderness. "Whoever gathered much had nothing left over, and whoever gathered little had no lack."[18] Paul was equating Christians' sharing with God's miracles of abundance in the Old Testament as if to indicate that we are now the instruments through which God provides enough to those in need. Our generosity is the miracle that will ensure each person has food to eat while wandering in the wilderness of the world.

The command to share is part of our common calling as the people of Christ. Every Christian in every time has been called to give, but some of us also have the particular calling to cultivate abundance through managing the distribution of these gifts. In Acts 6, we read that the church called seven people "of good repute, full of the Spirit and of wisdom" to distribute items to the poor.[19] Today Christ continues to call some of his servants to work with churches, charities, nonprofits, and government agencies to ensure the least among us have enough. They, too, manifest the abundance of Futureville in the wilderness of our world.

## THE CROSS

Scarcity creates fear. Not having enough food, water, or shelter has caused personal pain and devastating wars throughout history as people and societies strive to acquire what they need for life often at the expense of others. It is the scarcity of life itself, however, that provokes the most fear in us. Life was in abundance in Eden, but outside the garden it became a scarcity. For this rebellion, the Lord declared to the man, "You are dust, and to dust you shall return."[20]

The fear of our own mortality drives and directs the lives of most. We tenaciously try to retain our youth, or at least the appearance of it, in increasingly shocking ways. While caring for our bodies is affirmed as a virtue in Scripture, many pursue physical fitness from a desire to cheat death. Philosopher Simon Critchley noted that these cultural behaviors are also evident among Christians—those who claim belief in eternal life. He cited a survey showing 92 percent of Americans believe in God and 85 percent in heaven.

> But the deeper truth is that such religious belief, complete with a heavenly afterlife, brings believers little solace in the face of death. The only priesthood in which people really believe is the medical profession and the purpose of their sacramental drugs and technology is to support longevity, the sole unquestioned good of contemporary Western life.
>
> If proof were needed that many religious believers actually do not practice what they preach, then it can be found in the ignorance of religious teaching on death, particularly Christian teaching. . . . Christianity, in the hands of a Paul, an Augustine or a Luther, is a way of becoming reconciled to the brevity of human life and giving up the desire for wealth, worldly goods, and temporal power. . . . [But many Christians today] are actually leading desperate atheist lives bounded by a desire for longevity and a terror of [death].[21]

Rather than viewing the medical profession as a "priesthood" that appeases our great fear of death, Christians ought to honor those called by God into medicine and health care as cultivators of life. They are striving against death by seeking to bring wholeness to our bodies and cures to our diseases, but the temptation to deify doctors is tempered when we remember that their work can only delay, not defeat, our enemy. No one possesses the power to overcome death but God, who is the author of life.

Apart from those called to the health vocations, there are others who cultivate life in a more costly way. Some are given the specific call by God to sacrifice their own lives to save others. We have seen the heroism of police officers, soldiers, firefighters, and first responders, and we rightly honor their willingness to give their lives that others may live. Such sacrifice is often called upon amid the worst scenarios imaginable in the wilderness of the world, and this makes the sacrifice that much more glorious and powerful.

Anne Gordon, in *A Book of Saints*, tells of the sacrifice of Father Maximilian Kolbe. While he was a Nazi prisoner at Auschwitz in 1941, another inmate escaped from the camp. To deter more attempts, the Nazis ordered that ten prisoners were to die by starvation. After the ten were selected, Father Kolbe offered to take the place of one of the condemned. He was deprived of food in a bunker for two weeks and finally executed on August 14, 1941. Decades later, a survivor from Auschwitz told of the effect of Kolbe's sacrifice. The camp, he said, was a place of hopelessness, but Kolbe's willingness to die "a horrible death for the sake of someone not even related to him" filled them with hope that darkness would not ultimately prevail.

> Thousands of prisoners were convinced the true world continued to exist and that our torturers would not be able to destroy it. To say that Father Kolbe died for us or for that person's family is too great a simplification. His death was the salvation of thousands. . . . We were stunned by his act, which became for us a mighty explosion of light in the dark camp.[22]

Kolbe illustrates the unparalleled way self-sacrifice illuminates the present reality of Futureville. When one lays down his life for another, he is displaying immense love for the person saved. As Jesus declared, "Greater love has no one than this, that someone lay down his life for his friends."[23] Such sacrifice, however, also requires absolute faith in God's abundance. To accept death willingly is to trust that in God there is an abundance of life, that death will not have the last word, and that you will be rescued from its clutches to share in the unending life of God. To give up one's life is to believe that the wilderness of the world will not long endure, but the reality of Futureville, full of order, beauty, and abundance, will fill the cosmos with the resurrection power of Jesus Christ.

Such faith was evident in Jesus when he accepted death at the hands of sinners. We are told that it was "for the joy that was set before him" that he "endured the cross, despising the shame." Jesus trusted that after death he would be raised to life and be "seated at the right hand of the throne of God."[24] The resurrection is the ultimate manifestation of God's abundance and defeat of the world's scarcity. When Jesus rose he declared victory over death and opened the way that we might "have life and have it abundantly."[25]

In the cross of Christ we see the values and reality of Futureville most radiantly. By his death he has created order. He tore down the wall of hostility that had existed between people and made us one, and then reconciled us to God in one body through the cross.[26] At the cross Jesus also revealed the power of beauty. Others looked upon his tortured body and saw an ugly, meaningless waste. They wanted Jesus to do something practical. "Are you not the Christ?" they shouted. "Save yourself and us!"[27] Instead, he did what the world could only interpret as useless—he died. They did not have the eyes to see the beauty of his obedience. They could not see that by being lifted up on that Roman cross, he would draw all people to himself. The cross is also where the scarcity of death was swallowed up in the abundance of life. By overcoming the grave Jesus declared, and we with him, "O death, where is your victory? O death, where is your sting?"[28]

# TEN

# HOPE

WE BEGAN THIS JOURNEY TO FUTUREVILLE ON April 30, 1939, as thousands of Depression-era New Yorkers gazed upon the World of Tomorrow. They were lured across the river by the gleaming, white spire of the Trylon and received a glimpse of the city of the future inside the massive Perisphere. The '39 World's Fair inspired them with a vision of the future that ignited both hope and purpose—but like all visions it faded with time.

After two seasons the fair was closed and the buildings dismantled. One young resident of Queens said, "I wasn't prepared for the shock and disappointment of actually seeing the buildings and the Trylon and Perisphere being demolished when we drove by. I could not believe it. I was sad and angry.

The Trylon and Perisphere seemed so important, and they were so ubiquitous I never thought of them not being there."[1] The fair had to disappear. As long as it remained people would be content visiting the future rather than creating it; they would accept its facsimile of tomorrow while the real thing passed them by.

This is why, if they are to fulfill their purposes, all visions must dim to make space for a new reality to emerge. This explains why Jesus said to his disciples, "I tell you the truth: it is to your advantage that I go away."[2] Jesus came and inaugurated his kingdom of order, beauty, and abundance. He gave us a ravishing vision of the world reborn, but he ascended to the Father so that the Holy Spirit could come and empower those who believe to "do the works that I do; and greater works than these."[3] By leaving and giving us his Spirit, Jesus ensured that Futureville would be more than a vision. Through his people, reborn by the power of his resurrection, filled with his Spirit, and called to different works, Futureville would become a reality.

Like the '39 World's Fair, it is also time for our brief journey to the World of Tomorrow to fade. It has been brief and admittedly incomplete, but I trust you have a better understanding of the Christian vision of the future and how it shapes our purpose today. We have seen how the popular paths of evolution and evacuation fail to address our generation's jadedness, and why neither offers a comprehensive hope for a world lost in chaos, ugliness, and scarcity. We have also explored the biblical narrative that journeys from the garden, to the wilderness, to the city—Futureville, a flourishing world in which shalom reaches full maturity and where humanity dwells in unbroken unity with God.

We examined the way Jesus' resurrection began the new creation, and how the power of his resurrection is the only path to Futureville that offers a comprehensive hope for the cosmos. The magnitude of this hope led us to rediscover the abandoned theology of vocation. We found that purpose for Christ's people is not limited to social crusades or evangelism as narrowly defined by the paths of evolution and evacuation. Instead, Christ our Shepherd calls each of his sheep to a specific work in his world. Some are called to cultivate order, others beauty, and some abundance. In all these callings, and through the worship of the church, God is glorified as our world is given glimpses of Futureville's present reality and awaits that day when the cosmos is transformed as the voice of Christ declares, "Behold, I am making all things new."[4]

## THE END WITHOUT END

Until that glorious day, we remain in the wilderness of the world to both cultivate and capture glimpses of Futureville, but that task is not without its challenges. At the beginning I shared the two contrasting visions of the future I received as a child. Walt Disney's vision told me there was a "Great Big Beautiful Tomorrow" that would be built through human ingenuity and perpetual progress. That vision was shattered when my brother, Peter, died. Suddenly the future was no longer a vision to love and embrace, but merely one to fear and escape. Before Peter's death my childhood vision was one of naive optimism. After his death, like many in my generation, I embraced jaded cynicism.

My childhood experiences reflect the two dominant visions of the future held by many Christians—the paths of evolution and evacuation. Neither answered my need for hope or purpose, and the evidence shows my generation isn't responding to these visions either. It was later when I discovered the resurrection power of Jesus Christ that I discovered the path that could carry me all the way to the garden city of God. I embraced this Christian vision as an antidote to the naive humanism of the culture and cynical escapism of the church. Like the childhood vision I'd received from Disney, however, the shadow of death would come again to test my hope.

Eight years ago, my son, Isaac, whom I gave the middle name Peter in memory of my brother, was born prematurely. At first he thrived, but on Christmas Day his tiny body hemorrhaged and went into shock. We nearly lost him. For weeks he was kept alive with feeding tubes and blood transfusions. Eventually a consensus among the doctors started to form. Isaac's liver was failing, and even if he recovered, which was unlikely given his size, we were told children with his condition do not live to reach ten years old.

UCLA's basketball coach John Wooden said, "Adversity is the state in which man most easily becomes acquainted with himself."[5] In the months following Isaac's birth I became well acquainted with my anger. It was cruel and unfair, I told myself.

Once before I had experienced the pain that comes when a family loses a child. Now I must experience it again, but this time as the parent. The effects of Peter's death had reverberated through my parents' marriage for more than twenty years. How would Isaac's loss now change my life and marriage? Our son's illness also tested my hope in Christ. Was I a fool for believing this world could be anything but a wilderness? Was I mad for putting my hope in a God who would make all things new?

Looking back, that season did not cause me to question my Christian vision of the future. Instead, it caused me to question the usefulness of my Christian faith in the present. I still believed Christ would redeem all things and that Futureville would someday be reality, but with a sick and possibly dying child, a grieving wife, and an angry soul, I needed to see evidence of the garden city *now*. It wasn't enough for Christianity to offer a hope for tomorrow; my weakening faith—like the faith of so many others of my generation—was searching for evidence of God's renewal *today*. That became my prayer. I needed my eyes opened to see that God was with us and the power of his resurrection was at work in the ordinary brokenness of my world. He answered that prayer.

Isaac's symptoms seemed random and contradictory. For weeks doctor's struggled to understand what was happening inside his three-pound body. From this chaos they began to construct order. Using their skills and tools, they pieced together theories to explain his bleeding and his dysfunctional liver. They ran tests and patiently helped us understand what they were doing to our son. Some of the doctors, aware of their own limitations, prayed for Isaac. They recognized some things were beyond their ability to heal, and they humbly submitted to God. In the chaos they gave us glimpses of order.

As the weeks passed, Isaac's room in the neonatal intensive care unit filled with flowers, balloons, toys, and handmade blankets. Neighborhood kids and those from our church drew cards and pictures. The most beautiful sight, however, was arriving early in the morning to find Isaac being rocked in the arms of a volunteer. Women gave their time to hold infants in the NICU at night so that parents could rest. These surrogate grandmothers knew many of the children would not live long. It was a useless offering—and all the more beautiful as a result. In the ugliness of those days these wonderful women were glimpses of beauty.

Unlike the teddy bears and flowers, many of the gifts we received were very practical. We did not cook a meal for two months. Food arrived at our door every day from friends at church, and sometimes from strangers who'd heard about our need. Others cared for our older daughter so we could spend more time at the hospital. Anonymous checks came to assist with medical bills, and some came with notes explaining that God had placed it upon their hearts to help. In our scarcity these generous gifts were glimpses of abundance.

Through these people and many others who faithfully engaged their callings, God was helping me see the garden within the wilderness. He was showing me that my hope could withstand the reality of this fallen and fearsome world, and that he was at work making Futureville a reality even in the darkness of those days. I felt like John the Baptist racked with fear and doubt in Herod's dungeon asking Jesus, "Are you the one? Because everything I see tells me I was wrong." Jesus responded to John's doubt with kindness by sending John's friends back to him with reports of Futureville's reality. They helped John see what he could not see from his place in the shadows—the blind see, the deaf hear, and the lame walk. Similarly, Christ graciously offered me glimpses of Futureville even in the darkness of those days through doctors, friends, nurses, volunteers, and generous Christian brothers and sisters. As my vision was restored, I slowly found my anger dissolving and replaced with a peace I could not explain. This peace was most noticeable while waiting for the definitive test results on Isaac's liver. My wife and I sat by the phone all day. Before it rang we each expressed our trust in God, we affirmed our hope for the future regardless of the outcome, and we took comfort in the many ways we had already seen his kingdom through the faithful people manifesting order, beauty, and abundance all around us.

When the call came, we learned the test results were not good. Based on the doctors' explanation we accepted the fact that we were going to lose our son. I had given him the name Isaac before his illness and before I could know how his story would mirror the biblical character's. The Lord asked Abraham to sacrifice his only son, Isaac. Now he was asking me to surrender my Isaac as well, and like Abraham I could choose to trust his life to God or cling to anger, control, and fear.

That evening I found myself reading the words of Saint

Augustine in his book *The City of God*, where he described our eternal home as a place of perfect peace. Like our exploration of Futureville, Augustine emphasized the pervasive shalom that will fill the age to come. He wrote, "There we shall rest and see, see and love, love and praise. This is what shall be in the end without end."[6] The last phrase lodged in me—*the end without end*—and it soaked me with hope the way a summer downpour drenches the ground. The truth of it ran from my head to my toes, and I knew it was true in a way that went beyond knowledge. I knew the loss of Isaac would not be the end. We who belong to Christ do not believe in ends. We believe in the abundance of life. Isaac's life would never end, and neither would mine. As the ancient prayer of the church says, we believe in a "world without end." Having seen the evidence of God's kingdom in the present, and having a renewed hope in the unending kingdom yet to come, I found the faith to surrender Isaac to his care. My vision of tomorrow had given me strength for today.

Like Abraham at Moriah, I did not know that God had also provided a ram in the thicket for me. Days after the definitive test on Isaac's liver, a new specialist was brought onto his case. He offered a very different explanation for his symptoms and test results. He concluded that Isaac would recover and be perfectly healthy. No need for transplants, transfusions, or more tests. It seemed too good to be true, but time proved the specialist was right. Isaac did pull through. It was a long process with a number of setbacks, but today he is a perfectly healthy boy. The takeaway is not that outcomes are always positive, or that faith will spare us from the harsh realities of the wilderness of the world. Scripture, history, and our own experiences prove that is not the case.

Instead, we are to recognize that the wilderness will not endure forever. Our hope, rooted in the resurrection of Jesus Christ, is that a day is drawing nearer when the power of his resurrection will transform the world into Futureville, and the chaos, ugliness, and scarcity of the wilderness will be overcome by the order, beauty, and abundance of the garden city of God. Until then, we pray for the eyes to see the evidence of the garden all around us in the lives and faithfulness of Christ's people and their works, and we seek to cultivate these glimpses for others as we listen to and obey his calling for our lives. For in every age, no matter how optimistic or despairing, it is in Christ that we discover our hope—the One who is the same yesterday and today and forever.

# DISCUSSION QUESTIONS

## CHAPTER 1: VISION

1. In your experience, what has been the church's message about the future? How has this influenced what you believe matters most today?
2. What experiences, positive or negative, have most influenced the way you think about the future?
3. Do you believe the future will be better or worse than the present?
4. What matters more to God: being a missionary or being a gardener? Why?

## CHAPTER 2: CULMINATION

1. Think about teachings you've heard or read concerning the "end times" in the past. Describe the tone and emphases of these teachings. Did they fill you with hope, or fear, or both?
2. Why did God create humans? How did the description of the garden of Eden in this chapter shift the way you think about work?
3. *Shalom* describes the world when everything is right, whole, and flourishing. How did Jesus bring shalom during his earthly ministry? What might his example mean for the way we live today?
4. In Revelation, rather than seeing people ascending into heaven, John sees the city of God descending to the earth. What might be significant about this? How does this challenge your assumptions about the future?

## CHAPTER 3: EVOLUTION

1. Would you describe yourself as someone who believes humanity is gradually improving or steadily declining? Share your reasons.
2. Why are Christians, and particularly young people, attracted to messages about "changing the world"? What do these calls appeal to in you?
3. Who is most celebrated in your church or Christian

community? How is this communicated, and what messages are sent, directly or indirectly, as a result?

4. Share an example from your own experience of how Christians attempting to bring positive change in fact caused conflict and harm.

## CHAPTER 4: EVACUATION

1. How are Christians perceived in your community and in our society? How might this perception be the natural outcome of Christians believing the earth is doomed?
2. Share an experience of feeling guilty about not doing enough for God's mission or the church. What made you feel this way? How did you respond?
3. How do you see the value of safety being pursued by Christians? What is good about this? How might it be unhelpful?
4. Have you ever entertained the idea of leaving your present vocation to serve in a full-time ministry role? What sparked that idea? How would your community respond to such a decision?

## CHAPTER 5: RESURRECTION

1. Thinking back to God's original intent for humanity (see chapter 2), in what ways did Jesus fulfill Adam's original purpose?

2. What have you been taught about the significance of Jesus' resurrection in the past? Why does it matter to Christians?
3. If God is interested in redeeming our bodies and this earth, not simply taking souls to a nonphysical heaven, what are the implications for the way Christians live? How does this change the way we think about our purpose?
4. Speculate together. What do you think might endure from the present age for eternity? What will not endure? How does this challenge what you've been taught in the past about the future?

## CHAPTER 6: VOCATION

1. Do you live as if there is a division between secular and sacred work? How is this division evident in your own life and activities?
2. When did you first sense a calling to a specific task or work? What did you do to test that calling or determine whether it was a fit with your gifts and abilities?
3. Describe your experiences within the church or a Christian community. Share a time you felt empowered and equipped to accomplish what Christ is calling you to do in the world? Likewise, can you identify a time you felt controlled and used to further the agenda of the organization? How would you describe the leaders in each of these settings?
4. What is something your church could do to

communicate the value and dignity of each person's calling? How could you begin to do this in your own relationships with other Christians?

## CHAPTER 7: ORDER

1. How have relationships with others affected your relationship with God? Describe how your communion with God has influenced your relationship with another person. Why are we tempted to disconnect these two areas of our lives?
2. Share about someone in your life or community who has cultivated order. How has God used this person to bring shalom? How would things be worse if this person stopped using his or her gifts for the benefit of others?
3. What should matter more for Christians: alleviating present suffering or eternal suffering? What's wrong with this question?
4. Read Isaiah 58. What is the link between the way God's people worship and the cultivation of justice in the world? How might you apply the message of Isaiah 58 to your church or Christian community?

## CHAPTER 8: BEAUTY

1. Describe the last time you were arrested by beauty. What captured your attention? Why? How did it make you feel? What do you think makes God feel that way?

2. In what ways do you see Christians forcing beauty to submit to practicality? When is this a good thing, and how can it be taken too far?
3. Do you think it is ever acceptable for a church to spend money on purely aesthetic, impractical things? Why or why not?
4. Would you describe yourself more like the disciples or the woman in the story from Mark 14:3–9?
5. Share something you've done purely for the joy of it without any consideration of its practicality. Do you think God approves or disapproves of such behavior? Why?

## CHAPTER 9: ABUNDANCE

1. How might a business operate differently if those running it were interested in flourishing the community and not just making financial profits? What would the business measure other than the bottom line?
2. How do you feel when the offering is collected during worship gatherings in your church or Christian community? Why do you feel this way?
3. What fears do you have about giving your money away? What do your fears reveal about where you place your faith?
4. What is scarce in your community? How might you, together with others, begin to address this scarcity to create abundance?

# RECOMMENDED RESOURCES

IN CHAPTER 6, WE REDISCOVERED THE IMPORTANCE of vocation—the belief that God has called each of his children to a specific work in his world. As noted in that chapter, we can access our common callings through reading the Scriptures. Our individual, specific calling, however, is not as easily discovered. To know what we are called to cultivate in this world, and where, we must have three things:

1. A vibrant communion with God through faith in Christ and the presence of his Spirit.
2. A growing sense of humble self-awareness that acknowledges our gifts, abilities, weaknesses, and wounds.
3. A healthy set of relationships with Christian sisters and brothers who can confirm, and at times redirect, our sense of calling.

This book was written to help you reframe the way you think about the future, the world, and your purpose within it. Discerning your specific purpose, however, is an ongoing work I hope you will continue to investigate in communion with God and your church. To help you on that journey, here are a few resources I recommend:

Guinness, Os. *The Call: Finding and Filling the Central Purpose of Your Life* (Nashville: Thomas Nelson, 2003).

Palmer, Parker J. *Let Your Life Speak: Listening for the Voice of Vocation* (San Francisco: Jossey-Bass, 1999).

Smith, Gordon T. *Courage and Calling: Embracing Your God-Given Potential* (Downers Grove, IL: InterVarsity Press, 2011).

# ACKNOWLEDGMENTS

WITHOUT THE SUPPORT OF STEVE PERRY I NEVER would have had the space and flexibility to write this book. I appreciate your affirmation of my calling and ministry. Similarly, I am indebted to Dean Bruns for a meal at Smokin' Jakes in Arnold's Park, Iowa. That dinner was the answer to many prayers. Thank you for using your gifts so I could use mine.

*Futureville* is the second book I've written with the aid of Andy Brumbach and Dan Haase. Your feedback at our Friday morning meetings has shaped this book in countless ways. Thank you for sharing your artistic, literary, and spiritual gifts with me.

Joel Miller and the good people at Thomas Nelson, as well as Kathy Helmers and the team at Creative Trust Literary

Group, have been wonderful partners. Thank you for helping me share the message of *Futureville* with the church.

I am thankful for the encouragement of Brian and Cheryl Baird, Scottie May, Jim Lamott, and Tom and Mary Ellen Slefinger (who practically coauthored this book . . . *wink*). Our group has been a source of authenticity, caring, and joyful Christian community in my life.

Many of the people and stories of order, beauty, and abundance profiled in this book were discovered and first told by my gifted colleagues at *Christianity Today* behind the "This Is Our City" project: Andy Crouch, Katelyn Beaty, Nate Clarke, Christy Tennant Krispin, and Roxanne Wieman. Thank you for your efforts to tell stories of Christians seeking the flourishing of their communities.

I first met Walter Crutchfield, whose story appears in chapter 9, over an unusual meal in Cape Town, South Africa. Since then he's been a source of encouragement and support. Thank you for not only incarnating the messages of *With* and *Futureville*, but affirming my call to communicate them.

*Futureville* captures my thinking about how we are to relate to God's world. There is no doubt that the two people who most influenced my own vision of the world were my parents. As I get older and seek God for the wisdom to guide my own children, I grow increasingly grateful for values and instructions I received from my own mother and father. You showed me both the beauty and brokenness of this world, yet convinced me I would always be loved in the midst of it.

I remain ever thankful for my wife, Amanda. No matter what the future may hold, it brings me joy to know we will be yoked together as we work side by side in the garden of the Lord.

# NOTES

## CHAPTER 1: VISION

1. Barbara Cohen, Steven Heller, and Seymour Chwast, *Trylon and Perisphere* (New York: Harry N. Abrams, Inc., 1989), 17.
2. Chris Francescani, "'Life's Short. Get a Divorce.' Chicago Billboard Turns Heads," ABC News, May 7, 2007, http://abcnews.go.com/TheLaw/LegalCenter/story?id=3147979&page=1.
3. Paul Bradshaw, *Early Christian Worship* (Collegeville, MN: The Liturgical Press, 1996), 40.
4. "Five Myths About Young Adult Church Dropouts," Barna Group, November 16, 2011, http://www.barna.org/teens-next-gen-articles/534-five-myths-about-young-adult-church-dropouts.
5. Phil Vischer, "The Philosophical Implications of Talking Vegetables," speech delivered at Yale University, March 2, 2005, http://www.yale.edu/faith/downloads/x_vischer_veggie.pdf.
6. Ibid.
7. Stanley J. Grenz, *A Primer on Postmodernism* (Grand Rapids: Eerdmans, 1996), 13.

8. Jeff Kurtti, *Since the World Began: Walt Disney World—The First 25 Years* (Los Angeles: Disney Editions, 1996), 74.
9. Cathy Lynn Grossman, "Young Adults Aren't Sticking with Church," *USA Today*, August 6, 2007.
10. David Kinnaman and Gabe Lyons, *UnChristian* (Grand Rapids: Baker, 2007).
11. Psalm 90:17.
12. Hal Lindsey and Carole C. Carson, *The Late Great Planet Earth* (Grand Rapids: Zondervan, 1970).
13. Matthew 6:19–20.
14. Skye Jethani, *With: Reimagining the Way You Relate to God* (Nashville: Thomas Nelson, 2011).
15. Matthew 22:37–39.
16. 1 John 4:20.

## CHAPTER 2: CULMINATION

1. Revelation 4:1.
2. Genesis 1:1–2.
3. Genesis 2:8–9.
4. Genesis 2:15.
5. Genesis 1:27–28.
6. Genesis 1:28.
7. Genesis 3:5.
8. Genesis 1:28.
9. Friedrich Nietzsche, trans. Walter Kaufmann and R. J. Hollingdale, *The Will to Power* (New York: Vintage, 1967), 550.
10. Deuteronomy 4:34.
11. Exodus 35:30–35.
12. Exodus 40:34.
13. G. K. Chesterton, cited in Philip Yancey, *Soul Survivor: How Thirteen Unlikely Mentors Helped My Faith Survive the Church* (New York: Doubleday, 2001), chapter 3.
14. Kenneth I. Helphand, *Defiant Gardens: Making Gardens in Wartime* (San Antonio: Trinity University Press, 2008), 239.
15. Revelation 21:10–11.

16. The modern environmental movement also finds its roots in this time period. For more on the myth of a harmonious natural order without human involvement, I recommend reading Bill Birchard, *Nature's Keepers: The Remarkable Story of How the Nature Conservancy Became the Largest Environmental Group in the World* (New York: Jossey-Bass, 2005).
17. Genesis 1:28.
18. Revelation 21:18.
19. Revelation 21:3.
20. Revelation 21:1.
21. Revelation 21:23 NASB.
22. Revelation 22:3 NASB.

## CHAPTER 3: EVOLUTION

1. For example, Henry Blodget, "What Kills Us: The Leading Causes of Death from 1900–2010," *Business Insider*, June 24, 2012, http://www.businessinsider.com/leading-causes-of-death-from-1900-2010-2012-6?op=1.
2. This view of the future is known theologically as postmillennialism.
3. John F. Kennedy, American University speech, June 10, 1963, http://www.pbs.org/wgbh/americanexperience/features/primary–resources/jfk–university/.
4. William Wilberforce, diary entry on October 28, 1787, http://www.wilberforcecentral.org/wfc/wilberforce/.
5. H. G. Wells, Esq., "The Discovery of the Future," delivered in London, January 24, 1902; cited in Royal Institution of Great Britain, *Proceedings*, vol. 17, 1902–1904 (London: William Clowes and Sons, Ltd., 1906), 24.
6. H. G. Wells, *Mind at the End of Its Tether*, 1927.
7. Disney's Carousel of Progress was moved after the 1964 World's Fair to Disneyland in California, and then to the Magic Kingdom park at Walt Disney World in Florida in 1973. It has been updated many times, but much of the attraction remains the same as Walt's original version. It holds the record for the longest-running stage show in the history of American theater.

8. Charles Tilly, *The Politics of Collective Violence* (Cambridge University Press, 2003), 55.
9. Kevin Bales, *Disposable People* (Berkeley, CA: University of California Press, 1999), 8.
10. Andy Crouch, "Why We Can't Change the World," Q Talk, http://www.qideas.org/video/why–we–cant–change–the –world.aspx, accessed July 27, 2012.
11. George M. Marsden, *Understanding Fundamentalism and Evangelicalism* (Grand Rapids: Eerdmans, 1990), 59.
12. James Davidson Hunter interviewed by Christopher Benson, "Faithful Presence," *Christianity Today*, May 14, 2010, http: //www.christianitytoday.com/ct/2010/may/16.33.html ?start=1.
13. Jerry Falwell, *700 Club* broadcast, cited in "Falwell Apologizes to Gays, Feminists, Lesbians," CNN.com, September 14, 2001, http://archives.cnn.com/2001/US/09/14/Falwell.apology/.
14. Cal Thomas and Ed Dobson, *Blinded by Might: Why the Religious Right Can't Save America* (Grand Rapids: Zondervan, 2000), 46.
15. As reported by Gabe Lyons and David Kinnaman in *UnChristian: What a New Generation Really Thinks about Christianity . . . and Why It Matters* (Colorado Springs: Baker, 2007), 41, 91, 153.
16. David E. Campbell and Robert D. Putnam, "God and Caesar in America," *Foreign Affairs*, March/April 2012, http://www .foreignappfairs.com/articles/137100/david-e-campbell-and -robert-d-putnam/god-and-caesar-in-america.

## CHAPTER 4: EVACUATION

1. Theodore O. Wedel, "Evangelism—the Mission of the Church to Those Outside Her Life," *Ecumenical Review*, October 1953, 24.
2. The theological framework most often associated with this perspective is known as "premillennial dispensationalism." Dispensationalism was popularized in the twentieth century in the United States with the *Scofield Reference Bible*, which teaches

that God's relationship with humanity operates differently in various periods of history. It also advocates that God has a distinct plan for Israel apart from the church. Premillennialism believes Christ will return to earth before the 1,000-year reign of peace spoken of in Revelation 20. Taken together, these two theological systems teach that the church will be "raptured" away from the earth before a time of terrible tribulation occurs. With the church removed, Israel will once again be the focus of God's action in the world. Finally, Christ will return.

3. Chip Berlet, "End Times as a Growth Industry," PBS, *Frontline*, http://www.pbs.org/wgbh/pages/frontline/shows/apocalypse/readings/endtime.html.
4. The absence of white Christians was noticeable during the civil rights movement, a fact that has continued to hurt relations between Anglo and African American Christians in the United States.
5. The quote is often attributed to Oliver Wendell Holmes, but no original source has been located.
6. Kurt Seland, "The Post Rapture Survival Guide," RaptureReady.com, http://www.raptureready.com/rap34.html, accessed April 26, 2013.
7. Andy Crouch in "Cultivating Where We're Planted," interview by Derek R. Keefe, *Christianity Today*, September 8, 2008, http://www.ctlibrary.com/ct/2008/september/11.28.html, accessed March 13, 2013.
8. Matthew 9:37.
9. 1 Timothy 5:17.
10. Paul Vitello, "Taking a Break from the Lord's Work," *New York Times*, August 2, 2010, A1.
11. G. K. Chesterton, *Robert Browning*, 1923, chapter 8, http://www.online-literature.com/chesterton/robert-browning/8/.
12. Statistic based on 2006 reporting by The Association for Christian Retail, http://www.cbaonline.org/nm/timeline.htm, accessed March 11, 2013.
13. Dietrich Bonhoeffer, *Ethics* (New York: Touchstone, 1995), 198.
14. "Dan Cathy, Chick-Fil-A President, On Anti-Gay Stance:

'Guilty As Charged,'" *Huffington Post*, Gay Voices, July 17, 2012, http://www.huffingtonpost.com/2012/07/17/dan–cathy–chick–fil–a–president–anti–gay_n_1680984.html.
15. Robert Bork, *Slouching Towards Gomorrah: Modern Liberalism and American Decline* (New York: Harper, 1996), 334.
16. Theodore O. Wedel, "Evangelism—the Mission of the Church to Those Outside Her Life," *Ecumenical Review*, October 1953, 24.
17. Ibid.

## CHAPTER 5: RESURRECTION

1. Alcatraz and Devil's Island come to mind.
2. Nelson Mandela, *Long Walk to Freedom: The Autobiography of Nelson Mandela* (New York: Back Bay Books, 1995), 489–90.
3. Luke 7:19.
4. Luke 7:22.
5. Hebrews 10:25.
6. N. T. Wright, *Surprised by Hope: Rethinking Heaven, the Resurrection, and the Mission of the Church* (New York: HarperOne, 2008), 238.
7. 1 Corinthians 15:55.
8. 1 Corinthians 15:20.
9. 1 Corinthians 15:23.
10. 1 Corinthians 15:28.
11. Romans 8:18–23.
12. 1 Corinthians 15:28.
13. Colossians 1:18–20.
14. Revelation 21:1.
15. 2 Peter 3:12–13.
16. Romans 6:5.
17. 1 John 3:2.
18. Romans 8:21.
19. 1 Corinthians 15:42–44.
20. John 20:19.
21. Acts 1:9.
22. 1 Corinthians 15:51.

23. John 20:27.
24. 2 Corinthians 5:17.
25. Romans 8:21–22.
26. The fire imagery in 2 Peter 3:12–13, although assumed to be destructive, is consistent with the purifying purpose of fire Paul describes in 1 Corinthians 3:13 when speaking of the Day of Judgment.
27. 1 Corinthians 3:12–15.
28. Richard J. Mouw, *When the Kings Come Marching In: Isaiah and the New Jerusalem* (Grand Rapids: Eerdmans, 2002), 20.
29. Ibid., 24.
30. 1 Corinthians 15:28.

## CHAPTER 6: VOCATION

1. Eusebius, *Demonstrations of the Gospel*; cited in Os Guinness, *The Call* (Nashville: Thomas Nelson, 2003), 32.
2. Eusebius of Caesarea, *Demonstration of the Gospel*, in *The Proof of the Gospel: Being the Demonstratio Evangelica of Eusebius of Caesarea*, vol. 1, trans. W. J. Ferrar, (London: spck, 1920), 48–50.
3. Ephesians 4:28.
4. 1 Corinthians 10:31.
5. Martin Luther, *On the Babylonian Captivity of the Church*, 1520.
6. Abraham Kuyper, *Souvereiniteit in Eigen Kring* (Amsterdam: J. H. Kruyt, 1880), 35.
7. Os Guinness, *The Call* (Nashville: Thomas Nelson, 2003), 31.
8. If you are confused by this highest calling to live with God, I recommended reading my previous book, *With: Reimagining the Way You Relate to God* (Nashville: Thomas Nelson, 2011).
9. Ron Fournier and Sophie Quinton, "How Americans Lost Trust in Our Greatest Institutions," *The Atlantic*, April 20, 2012, http://www.theatlantic.com/politics/archive/2012/04/how-americans-lost-trust-in-our-greatest-institutions/256163/.
10. Lydia Saad, "U.S. Confidence in Organized Religion at Low

Point," Gallup Politics, July 10, 2012, http://www.gallup.com/poll/155690/confidence–organized–religion–low–point.aspx.

11. Dallas Willard, *The Spirit of the Disciplines: Understanding How God Changes Lives* (New York: HarperOne, 1999), 214.
12. Ephesians 4:11–13.
13. John 21:22.
14. Matthew 9:37.
15. Matthew 9:38.
16. Ephesians 2:10.
17. Dorothy Sayers, "Why Work?," *Letters to a Diminished Church: Passionate Arguments for the Relevance of Christian Doctrine* (Nashville: Thomas Nelson, 2004), 131. Essay available at http://faith-at-work.net/Docs/WhyWork.pdf.

## CHAPTER 7: ORDER

1. Katelyn Beaty, "Portland's Quiet Abolitionists," *Christianity Today*, November 2011, http://www.christianitytoday.com/ct/2011/november/portlandabolitionists.html.
2. Quoted in *M. C. Escher's Legacy: A Centennial Celebration*, eds. Doris Schattschneider and Michele Emmer (Berlin: Springer Press, 2005), 71.
3. Genesis 1:28.
4. N. T. Wright, *New Dictionary of Theology*, eds. David F. Wright, Sinclair B. Ferguson, and J. I. Packer (Downers Grove, IL: InterVarsity Press, 1997), 590–92, s.v. "Righteousness," available at http://ntwrightpage.com/Wright_NDCT_Righteousness.htm.
5. Joslyn Baker quoted by Katelyn Beaty, "Portland's Quiet Abolitionists," *Christianity Today*, November 2011.
6. Shoshon Tama-Sweet quoted by Katelyn Beaty, "Portland's Quiet Abolitionists," *Christianity Today*, November 2011.
7. John Stott and Ajith Fernando, *Christian Mission in the Modern World* (Downers Grove, IL: InterVarsity Press, 2008).
8. Ibid., 41.
9. Ibid., 43.
10. Romans 4:5.

11. Ron Sider, "An Open Letter to This Generation, Part 1," *Relevant*, March 14, 2011, http://www.relevantmagazine.com/god/deeper-walk/features/24972-an-open-letter-to-this-generation-pt-1.
12. John Piper, "Bible Exposition: Ephesians 3—John Piper (Part 2)—Cape Town 2010," http://www.youtube.com/watch?v=1a5V1O4M4rU, accessed April 26, 2013.
13. John Stott and Ajith Fernando, *Christian Mission in the Modern World* (Downers Grove, IL: InterVarsity Press, 2008), 45.
14. Revelation 21:3.
15. Jonathan Edwards quoted in *A Young Person's Guide to Wisdom* by Jeff Claiborne (Camarillo, CA: Xulon Press, 2012), 124.
16. Amos 5:24.
17. Isaiah 1:23.
18. Isaiah 58:6–8.
19. Matthew 5:23–24.
20. Matthew 6:14–15.
21. Ephesians 2:15–16.
22. 1 John 4:20.
23. 1 Corinthians 11:18, 20–22.
24. Galatians 3:28 RSV.
25. 1 Corinthians 11:27 RSV.
26. 1 Corinthians 11:27.
27. Desmond Tutu, *Hope and Suffering* (Glasgow: Fount, 1983), 134–35.


## CHAPTER 8: BEAUTY


1. Harrison Higgins, quoted by Nathan Clarke, "Furniture Fit for the Kingdom" (video), *Christianity Today*, May 1, 2012, http://www.christianitytoday.com/thisisourcity/richmond/furniturefit.html, accessed December 4, 2012.
2. Genesis 2:8–9.
3. Genesis 1:3–5.
4. Genesis 1:6–8.
5. Genesis 1:9–10.
6. Romans 1:20.

7. G. K. Chesterton, *Collected Works of G. K. Chesterton: The Illustrated London News, 1923–1925* (San Francisco: Ignatius Press, 1990), 186.
8. Exodus 35:30–35.
9. G. K. Chesterton, *Collected Works of G. K. Chesterton: The Illustrated London News, 1923–1925* (San Francisco: Ignatius Press, 1990), 186.
10. Sean Brennan, "Bills Receiver Steve Johnson Appears to Blame God in Tweet for Awful Dropped Pass against Steelers," *New York Daily News*, November 29, 2010, http://www.nydailynews.com/sports/football/bills-receiver-steve-johnson-appears-blame-god-tweet-awful-dropped-pass-steelers-article-1.450613.
11. Psalm 27:4.
12. Rachel Kaplan and Stephen Kaplan, *The Experience of Nature: A Psychological Perspective* (Cambridge: Cambridge University Press, 1989).
13. Deborah Franklin, "How Hospital Gardens Help People Heal," *Scientific American*, March 19, 2012, http://www.scientificamerican.com/articlecfm?id=nature-that-nurtures.
14. W. David O. Taylor, ed., *For the Beauty of the Church: Casting a Vision for the Arts* (Colorado Springs: Baker, 2010), 36.
15. NPR Fresh Air interview, "Crushing Eastern Europe—Behind the 'Iron Curtain,'" *NPR*, November 8, 2012, http://m.npr.org/news/Books/164632546. Transcript provided by NPR, copyright NPR.
16. Daniel A. Siedell, "Why Mako Fujimara Left New York City for the Country," *Christianity Today*, September 25, 2012, http://www.christianitytoday.com/thisisourcity/newyork/why-mako-fujimura-left-new-york-city-for-country.html.
17. Mark 14:3–6.
18. W. David O. Taylor, ed., *For the Beauty of the Church: Casting a Vision for the Arts* (Colorado Springs: Baker, 2010), 40.
19. Daniel Buttry, "Vedran Smajlović: The Brave Cellist of Sarajevo Still Moves the World," Read the Spirit, http://www.readthespirit.com/explore/vedran-smajlovic-cellist-of

-sarajevo-still-moves-the-world, excerpted from Daniel Buttry, *Blessed Are the Peacemakers* (Detroit: David Crumm Media, 2011), 305–308.

20. Kenneth I. Helphand, *Defiant Gardens: Making Gardens in Wartime* (San Antonio: Trinity University Press, 2008), 1.
21. George Eisen, *Children and Play in the Holocaust: Games Among the Shadows* (Amherst: University of Massachusetts Press, 188), 8.
22. Christy Tennant Krispin, "A Growing Hunger for a Local Voice: Sara Groves and Family Open Art House in St. Paul," *Christianity Today*, June 26, 2012, http://www.christianitytoday.com/thisisourcity/7thcity/open-art-house.html, accessed December 4, 2012.
23. Roberta Ahmanson, "Presentation to the Global Executive Leadership Forum," Cape Town, South Africa, October 2010.
24. Ibid.
25. Revelation 21:4.
26. Kenneth I. Helphand, *Defiant Gardens: Making Gardens in Wartime* (San Antonio: Trinity University Press, 2008), 248.

## CHAPTER 9: ABUNDANCE

1. Nathan Clarke, "Business Declares the Glory of God," (video), *Christianity Today*, October 8, 2012, http://www.christianitytoday.com/thisisourcity/phoenix/business-declares-glory-of-god.html, accessed December 21, 2012.
2. St. Thomas Aquinas, *Summa Theologica Volume 2* (Part II, First Section) (New York: Cosimo Classics, 2013), 773.
3. Revelation 21:25.
4. Quoted by Walter Brueggemann, "The Liturgy of Abundance, The Myth of Scarcity," *Christian Century*, March 24, 1999.
5. Exodus 16.
6. Isaiah 55:1.
7. Revelation 22:17.
8. Walter Brueggemann, "The Liturgy of Abundance, the Myth of Scarcity," *Christian Century*, March 24–31, 1999, http://www.religion-online.org/showarticle.asp?title=533.

9. Nathan Clarke, "Business Declares the Glory of God," *Christianity Today*, October 8, 2012, http://www.christianitytoday.com/thisisourcity/phoenix/business-declares-glory-of-god.html.
10. Morgan Feddes, "Calling All Callings: Amy Sherman on 'Kingdom Calling,'" *Christianity Today*, February 9, 2012, http://www.christianitytoday.com/ct/2012/january/amy-sherman-kingdom-calling.html.
11. Matthew Philips, "Goldman's Dubious Deals: Is This 'God's Work'?" *BusinessWeek*, March 7, 2012, http://www.businessweek.com/articles/2012-03-07/goldmans-dubious-deals-is-this-gods-work.
12. Chris Irvine, "Goldman Sachs Boss: 'Bankers Do God's Work,'" *The Telegraph*, November 8, 2009; http://www.telegraph.co.uk/finance/newsbysector/banksandfinance/6524972/Goldman–Sachs–boss–bankers–do–Gods–work.html.
13. Mehul Srivastava, "Why Can't India Feed Its People?," *BusinessWeek*, November 21, 2012, http://www.businessweek.com/articles/2012-11-21/why-cant-india-feed-its-people.
14. Dorothy Sayers, "Why Work?," *Letters to a Diminished Church: Passionate Arguments for the Relevance of Christian Doctrine* (Nashville: Thomas Nelson, 2004), 131.
15. Proverbs 11:10 NIV.
16. Acts 4:34.
17. 2 Corinthians 8:14.
18. 2 Corinthians 8:15; quoting Exodus 16:18.
19. Acts 6:1–6.
20. Genesis 3:19.
21. Simon Critchley, *The Book of Dead Philosophers* (New York: Vintage Books, 2008), 247–48.
22. Anne Gordon, *A Book of Saints* (New York: Random House, 1994), 77.
23. John 15:13.
24. Hebrews 12:2.
25. John 10:10.
26. Ephesians 2:16.

27. Luke 23:39.
28. 1 Corinthians 15:55.

## CHAPTER 10: HOPE

1. Stephen R. Langenthal, quoted in Barbara Cohen, Steven Heller, and Seymour Chwast, *Trylon and Perisphere* (Harry N. Abrams, Inc.: New York, 1989).
2. John 16:7.
3. John 14:12.
4. Revelation 21:5.
5. Pat Williams, *Coach Wooden: The 7 Principles That Shaped His Life and Will Change Yours* (Grand Rapids: Revell, 2007), 178.
6. Augustine, *The City of God* (Random House Digital, 2010), 867.

# ABOUT THE AUTHOR

SKYE JETHANI (@SKYE_JETHANI) IS THE EXECUTIVE editor of the Leadership Media Group at *Christianity Today* and also contributes regularly to *Relevant*, *The Huffington Post*, and radio programs around the country. His blog (www.skyejethani.com) was awarded second prize for the best Christian blog by the ECPA. He is a frequent speaker at Catalyst and Q. Skye earned a masters of divinity degree in 2001 from Trinity Evangelical Divinity School in Deerfield, Illinois. He and his wife, Amanda, currently live in Wheaton, Illinois, with their three children, Zoe, Isaac, and Lucy.